When we intend for rain,
instead of talking about how dry it is,
we envision it raining.

When we intend that we are happy and healthy,
instead of telling everyone our problems,
we envision ourself happy and well.

When we intend that we are abundant,
instead of telling everyone about our hard times,
we envision having enough to spare and share.

When we intend for fair and honest leadership,
instead of obsessing on poor politics,
we see our elders standing for the Highest Good.

When we see things in a favorable light,
we're no longer reinforcing our own problems;
we're no longer complicit in our own suffering.

.

And when we see things in their brightest light,
we put the Law of Attraction to its highest and best use;
we marry the Law and the Highest Good together.

What will bring about a mass change of consciousness is enough people thinking and believing and knowing in the Highest Good.

Lee Ching

It's all about win-win.

BJ

The Highest Good
Handbook

Love, Life, Liberty
and
the Pursuit of Happiness

Tony Burroughs

Highest Light House

The Highest Good Handbook
Love, Life, Liberty & the Pursuit of Happiness

Copyright © 2018 by Tony Burroughs

Printed in the United States of America

ISBN: 978-0-9819020-6-7

Dedicated to all who carry the pure intention
of everyone awakening to the Highest Good

Published by:
Highest Light House
105 Highland Avenue
Pagosa Springs, CO 81147
Book Orders: 858-200-5200
info@highestlighthouse.com
www.highestlighthouse.com

For more information about
The Intenders of the Highest Good
visit www.intenders.com

For more information about the author
visit www.tonyburroughs.net

The Highest Good is different for everyone.
For the caring, it brings its gifts.
For the angry, it brings its lessons.
For all, it brings its opportunities.

"Each of you has different challenges and goals that you've set for yourself before you came into this life. One person's soul's purpose can be entirely different from another's. One may need to experience great wealth and all its trappings in order to balance out lifetimes of hardship, while another may have arranged to be poverty stricken in order to balance out lifetimes of dissipation and addiction that often go along with being wealthy.

"In each and every instance, the Highest Good is working to help your soul come back into alignment with the calling you set for yourself before you came into your current body. Regardless of outer appearances, the Highest Good is always nudging you back toward your reason for being here."

When you step into your calling,
all things open up for you,
and the way is made clear for you
to do that which you have come here to do.

Table of Contents

*Take our Fun Final Exam on page 214 and receive your
Certificate of Alignment with the Highest Good Award
to hang on your wall.*

Preface

"You always have your intentions," he said. "You may have times with little or no cash, but you always have your intentions. You always have the ability to manifest whatever you need by intending it." Lee Ching said this to me right before I boarded the plane for the mainland to leave my comfy tropical home in Hawaii. All I had in my pocket at the time was $37 ... and my intentions.

These parting words from my mentor were my inspiration for setting out to live by manifesting, to live by making intentions and trusting that everything I needed would be there for me whenever I needed it. As a result, I've lived my entire adult life on that trust, testing the Law of Attraction / Intention Process every chance I got. I've never taken a full-time job; I just intended my way through life. Scary? You bet. Frustrating at times? Of course. In truth, there were moments when I wasn't sure whether it was working or not. But, looking back, I can see that everything that happened along the way was for my Highest Good.

Everyone has a calling in this life.
Do you know what yours is?

The stories in this book come from my personal experiences with the Intenders. We started our Intenders of the Highest Good community over twenty-five years ago in Pahoa, Hawaii, and since then we've seen thousands of people from all over the world manifest their intentions in our Intenders Circles and have their dreams come true. At first, we didn't know what we were doing; we were just four friends (Tina, Mark, Betsy, and me) meeting weekly and intending to help one another in anyway we could. It wasn't long, though, before five of our friends joined our little group and, for the next year, we were nine Intenders. Then, one Sunday evening, thirty-five people showed up!

That which you are reaching toward
is also reaching out to you.

The Intenders took off from there, with our second circle starting up in Kona, and our third in Petaluma, CA. What with the sudden interest and new circles being added every week, I moved from the Big Island to the San Francisco Bay Area (with only the afore-mentioned $37 in my pocket), and, long story short, within a year, seventeen Intenders Circles were active in Northern California—and it flashed across the country from there. Now, you'll find Intenders Circles in countries all across the globe, and if you were to ask us today what caused this wondrous phenomenon, we would all, without exception, point to the Highest Good.

In the beginning, we watched in awe as our fellow Intenders came back every week to tell their stories of success after having stated their intentions into our circle the week before. New mates, new jobs, extra money, unexpected travel —we saw it all. With each week that passed, we became less skeptical and more trusting in the amazing process we were working with. The more we included the Highest Good in with our intentions, the more we knew we were onto something very special.

You came into this life with your desires.
The more skilled you become at fulfilling them,
the happier you will be.

As it turned out, we were marrying the process of deliberate manifestation with the Highest

Good and bringing them into a community setting where people could intend and manifest together in groups. Previous to this, we'd been concerned about whether to share our intentions aloud with our friends and neighbors. We'd been told that others might try to undermine or sabotage our intentions, and that we should keep them to ourselves. However, when my friend and mentor, Lee Ching, told us about the Highest Good phrase, and we started including it in our intention-making, we realized right away that we'd found a way to share our dreams and desires with others without the danger of our intentions being compromised in any way. We called it the world's greatest insurance policy, and we learned to never say our intentions without including the Highest Good phrase:

"I intend that,
in order for my intentions to manifest,
they must serve the Highest Good of the
Universe, myself, and everyone concerned."

From this point on, we were free to take advantage of the strength that comes from working together. We'd created a way to gather in groups and manifest as One, instead of trying to do all of our self-empowerment work by ourselves. The Highest Good opened the door and, together, we stepped through into the grace and power of a conscious community.

Tony Burroughs
11/11/17

Introduction

My relationship with the Highest Good has taken me on the wildest ride imaginable. Over the course of my adult life, I've gone from being an advocate, to acting as an ambassador, and finally to becoming an unshakeable activist on its behalf. The stories are many, and you, my friend, will be reading some of the ones that influenced me the most over the years. It all began in 1994 when I heard the words "the Highest Good" for the first time. My friend, Tina, and I were chatting about how to get the most out of our lives, when she casually mentioned something about lining up with the Highest Good. These words instantly resonated so deeply in me that it felt like the clouds parted, and a clarity I'd never known opened up before me. Prior to this, I'd never really had a reference point when faced with the choices of life. I'd been brought up in a world where win-lose, profit and loss, and the "me first" American way of life predominated. However, this way of life never felt quite right to me. Something in my core called out for balance, a shift back to *win-win*, where my fellow travelers' benefit is considered as much or more than my own personal goals and desires.

The Highest Good continued to intrigue me. I thought about it everyday, but I still didn't know what it meant. I was going on a feeling, *a sweet feeling*, but I had no working definition for it. My only point of reference was something Lee Ching said after one of our early Intenders Circles.

Not long after we'd begun our fledgling intention-making circle, we started adding the Highest Good phrase after stating our gratitudes and intentions. Up to this point, it felt like something was missing in our intentions; we certainly didn't want to be manifesting anything that harmed or impeded anyone else's path in life. Not only that, but I felt that we needed a foolproof method, a safety valve, in order to make sure that our intentions were pure, and that we weren't bringing unwanted experiences into our lives.

When I asked Lee Ching about this, his gentle reply was to have a great effect on our entire group, as well as the lives of all those we touched from then on. "Tony,"he said, **"what you say is what you get. When you include the Highest Good phrase at the end of your intentions, according to the Law of Attraction, it insures that *if your intention is for the Highest Good, it will manifest—and if it's not for the Highest Good, it won't manifest."***

Two and a half decades later, I've found Lee Ching's words to be timeless and true. Indeed, I've seen so many of my fellow Intenders manifest their dreams using the Highest Good phrase—and I've seen many times when my friends' intentions weren't manifested because, as it turned out, they clearly weren't in the highest and best interests of everyone concerned. I've even witnessed instances where newcomers would purposely leave off the Highest Good phrase when they stubbornly wanted their intention to manifest, whether it was for the Highest Good or not. But, in the long run, the ensuing *miscreation* was always disastrous.

Without exception, they wished they'd never made that intention in the first place.

(Throughout this book, you'll come across several passages entitled, *"Mainstream Miscreations."* A *miscreation* is an unloving manifestation that doesn't serve you or anyone else, and doesn't end up with the outcomes you're intending for. We recommend that you pay close attention to these *miscreations*, so that you'll be less apt to manifest them in your life from now on.)

You can create your life
to be any way you want it.

As I got more proficient at making my intentions, I realized that the Highest Good was at work in two areas of my life at the same time: 1) in my personal life, and 2) in the world at large. Through my experiences with the Intenders I'd already begun to develop a personal definition for it. *I knew I was in alignment with the Highest Good when I was honoring my soul's calling, and when I stayed on track with my purpose for coming here.* This definition was working like a charm in

15

my personal life, but how would I know when our world is lined up with the Highest Good? How is the Highest Good at work in a worldly sense? These questions puzzled me until the answer came from the most reliable of sources: the Founding Fathers: the Framers of the US Constitution. In creating one of the most powerful and poignant documents of our time, they emphatically stated that *"Life, Liberty and the Pursuit of Happiness"* took precedence over all other guidelines.

LIFE—that we are all allowed to live out our lives to full completion without the interference of others; *LIBERTY*—that we are free to explore, experience, and evolve to our highest potential, as long as we do not impede the paths of our fellowmen and women; *THE PURSUIT OF HAPPINESS*—that we recognize and acknowledge that we're all seeking our innermost joy and happiness in everything we do, and that life will inherently lead us there if we are left alone to follow the promptings of our heart.

At last I had a worldly definition, but something was still missing. It still didn't feel complete to me. Surely, the Founding Fathers would roll over in their graves at the thought of how much fighting had gone on since they penned their beautiful *Declaration of Independence.* They'd see that we've been warring with our neighbors in order to maintain *Life, Liberty and our Pursuit of Happiness* throughout all of recorded history, and not once have we experienced a true and lasting peace. In point of fact, fear and fighting have only continued to make matters worse for us, while love is the only thing that could possibly bring us relief. Obviously, we needed to find a new approach to resolving our worldly problems—*and now I knew what it was!* We'd have to go beyond *Life, Liberty and the Pursuit of Happiness,* and add *Love* to our definition for the Highest Good. For only through learning to *Love* and forgive our fellow travelers, whether they're our friends *or our enemies*, will we ever experience our Highest Good.

We intended for the Highest Good,
and it took us to Love.

Love works when we start within and work our way outward from there. This means that before we can change our outer world, we'll need to do

17

the work inside us first; we need to Love ourselves before we can Love anyone else. That said, in order to deal with the perpetual human condition, with its rampant fear, inequality, slavery, debt, disease creation, false enemies, wars, and environmental challenges, we'll first need to address the issues inside of us that are creating these outer, worldly conditions.

Naturally, we will be touching on these worldly challenges throughout this book, *but not with an attitude of judgment or blame,* for fear and judgment have been the cause of our worldly problems since time began. In the pages ahead, we'll activate some new tools that don't involve fearing and fighting. We'll go beyond our old ways and learn to *"overlook"* all judgment, blame, wrongdoing, and guilt, just as *Love* would have us do. We'll explore *"the new forgiveness"* and learn how we can have a positive effect on our world by working within our own being, for that is where our real challenges reside. This is the first lesson the Highest Good would have us learn: that it's all happening in our mind, and that is where the real work is to be done.

Your joy, your comfort, and your security
all come from inside of you.

The Highest Good is the key to our personal and our collective human fulfillment. It's our best friend, guiding us every step of the way, if we will but call it forth into our lives. The information and stories that follow are deliberately designed to provide you with relief from both your personal and collective challenges in the form of an alignment with the Highest Good. Of course, there may be times when the Highest Good will bring some temporary discomfort (more on that later), but this is only because *Love, Life, Liberty, and the Pursuit of Happiness* are not being honored, and you need to bring balance back into your life. Isn't that what you really want for yourself? In your heart of hearts, don't you really want to experience *Love* at its finest? Don't you really want to live more fully and freely, more happily and healthfully, more inspired everyday? The Highest Good promises all this to you and more, and all you have to do is line up with it and be open to receive.

Two Mentors

~ BJ ~

Before going any further, let's introduce you to my two mentors: BJ and Lee Ching. I met my first mentor, BJ, back in the early 1970s, at a party down the country road from where I was living in Kona, Hawaii. Tall and rugged, but extremely wise, BJ had a magnetism, an unseen force, that instantly attracted me to him. I invited him up to my farm and, in short, he built a coffee shack through the trees from mine and, over the next 18 years, we worked together as he passed along his knowledge to me. Truly a jack-of-all-trades, it seemed like there was nothing BJ couldn't build or fix. His specialty, however, was communication, and, whenever he decided to pass along information to someone else, there was no trick in the book he wouldn't use in order to get his message across.

BJ believed that mere talking didn't always communicate ideas effectively; he thought experience was the best teacher. As a result, whenever I had a challenge in my life, BJ would use it to teach me one facet or another of the knowledge he was sharing. Little did I realize at the time that *it was BJ, behind the scenes, setting up my challenges,* so I would have to learn the lessons he was teaching.

I remember one Thanksgiving awhile back when I asked BJ how he came to be so detached from the people and dramatic situations going on around him. I even said I envied his ability to remain so calm in the face of challenging problems. He thought for a moment, and then changed the subject, suggesting that I take on the job of putting together the Thanksgiving dinner for that year.

I agreed and immediately went out and spent the last of my money on a nice turkey and all the trimmings. Two days later, on Thanksgiving, I baked the turkey along with all the candied yams, stuffing, cranberry sauce, etc. I even splurged on a pumpkin pie and a bottle of holiday wine.

After I had the country kitchen smelling wonderful, with all the trimmings on the table, and the turkey just coming out of the oven, BJ showed up and said, "Now, Tony, if you really want to learn something about your attachments, don't eat a bite." And with that, he quickly excused himself, leaving me to sit there alone

*and decide whether to eat that beautiful dinner, or
confront my attachment to the meal set out on the
table in front of me—a meal I'd paid for and prepared
myself, a meal that smelled so good I couldn't believe
it! What would you have done?*

~ Lee Ching ~

My next mentor was just the opposite. Lee Ching
was kind and gentle in everything he taught, never
raising his voice, or pushing my buttons (like BJ),
or saying an uncaring word. As the masculine
archetype of mercy, and companion to Quan Yin
(the feminine archetype of compassion), he always
exuded a deep feeling of love for me, no matter
how troubled I was at the time. In fact, sometimes
that feeling would arise from a few simple words
he'd say that opened my heart and brought tears
to my eyes. It was like being in the presence of
Jesus Christ, or a great ascended master.

*I recognized my mentor, Lee Ching, the minute we
met. Even though he was not in a body of his own,
I felt him like no other spiritual being I'd ever felt,*

with the exception of Jesus. The feeling I have when Lee Ching is present is similar to the feeling I have when the Christ is present, yet it carries a calm, merciful patience that is distinct to him.

Although some masters prefer to teach by using "tough love" methods, Lee Ching rarely resorted to using harshness. Unlike BJ, whose methods were designed to provoke an immediate response, Lee Ching's words carried the gentle assurance that everything will happen in its perfect timing. As a result, I never felt any pressure from him. In truth, not once, in over twenty-five years, have I felt anything but a deep spiritual love coming from Lee Ching.

I met Lee Ching through my good friend, Tina Stober. In fact, he took a bit of getting used to at first because, as I said, he was not in his own body at this time, but had to "come through" a messenger or medium, namely Tina. During the first year of our relationship, I got together with Tina and Lee Ching at every opportunity. Then one day, he said that he wasn't exclusive to Tina, and that he'd "come through" me, in my writing, if I intended it. And, true to his word, a few days later, he did.

It was Lee Ching who taught us all about the power of intention. In our original Intenders Circle, he told us that anytime we were about to do anything, it was wise for us to *"set our course"* for what was to follow. He said that by saying our intentions in the morning, we were setting a direction for our day—while those who got out of bed, had a cup of coffee, and went straight to work or play got whatever might happen to them that day. This, he said, was one of the differences between being conscious or unconscious in life.

As it turned out, Lee Ching's gentle teachings became the foundation for the Intenders of the Highest Good. Little did we realize 25 years ago that our small Intenders Circle would give birth to a worldwide community. But Lee Ching knew it all along, having told us, early on, that a time was coming, years into the future, when our Intenders Circles would grow and have their greatest impact when they are needed most.

Clearly, that time is now.

In the midst of all the strife and craziness,
millions are waking up to the Highest Good.

The Highest Good Guides

To Line up with the Highest Good,

~Remember~

Life is precious
The Earth is beautiful
We're meant to play
We're meant to be happy
Everything is all right if we believe it is
Good friends are better than gold
Our family is larger than we think
People are different but equal
Forgiving is it's own reward
Freedom is inside us
Gifts are ours for the asking
Prayers and intentions work
See and feel your intentions manifesting
Miracles are our birthright
Trust gives us power
Ideals give us direction
Optimism gives us success
Moderation refreshes us

The Highest Good Guides

To Line up with the Highest Good,

~Remember~

Communication connects us
Adversity corrects us
Non-violence heals us
It's all in present time
It's all in perfect order
Love is all around us
We're more than we think we are
Oneness is our next step
The Highest Good will set us free

*Note: The chapter titles and contents that follow are based on guidelines that have helped us over the years remember to line up with the Highest Good. We've even created a poster entitled **"The Highest Good Guides"** that is designed to help you line up with the Highest Good, as well. It's free and you can download our 8.5x11 **"Highest Good Guides"** color poster at: http://www.highestlighthouse.com/highestgood.html*

{Remember}
Life Is Precious

If you've ever survived a life-threatening situation, then you know that life is a precious gift. It allows us to experience all the wonder and grandeur of our beautiful Earth; it gives us opportunities to love and be loved by others; it provides an ideal setting for us to learn, and grow, and fulfill our soul's purpose. Without it, we would have to look elsewhere to find the joys and sorrows, the pleasures and pains, and the amazing array of adventures that are available to us only if we are alive.

Think about it. If you didn't have a body, you couldn't enjoy tasting delicious foods or listening to good music; you couldn't savor the companionship of good friends; you couldn't feel the excitement of driving a car, the serenity of a walk in the woods, the intimacy and passion of making love. None of these are available to us if we don't have a body to enjoy them with.

Sadly, the precious gift of life is undermined nowadays by those who don't value its splendor. They spread the insane idea that this world is such a bad place to be that there's really no reason to stay here. As a result, many people who are temporarily unhappy believe these crazy ideas and want to check out before their time. But for those who are resilient and have the strength to bounce back from the face of adversity and hardship, there's a whole world out there filled with people who want to help put their fellow travelers back on the path of happiness and creativity. If we will but open up, even a little, we'll find that there are people who love us and want us to love them. Indeed, there are people all around us who need to be loved just as much as we do—and if we're willing to lift ourselves up and out of our unhappiness, and we go out and help someone else, we'll soon discover something we may never have known existed. We may discover our reason for being here.

If you've lost hope
and thoughts of despair are weighing you down,
go help someone else who needs it,
and you will be helped in return.

One day when I was homeless and had nowhere to go, my cell phone rang, and it was a friend of my good friend, Veronica, telling me the she (Veronica) was sick and didn't have long to live. Although I was a thousand miles away, I immediately hopped in my car (which I was living in at the time), drove across three states, and knocked on Veronica's door.

When I opened the door, she was lying there on the living room couch, unable to get up on her own. There was nobody there to help her, so I said, "If you need me, I'll stay here with you for as long as you like."

Well, her eyes opened wide and she nodded, but it wasn't the nod that touched me; it was the feeling that overcame me as I stepped into the room. My heart opened like it hadn't in so long I couldn't remember. It was one of the most precious moments of my life.

From that day on, until the day I held her hand four months later as she was making her transition, I did everything I possibly could to make her life more comfortable. I fed her, bathed her, clothed her, and kept the movies going to keep her entertained. I can't explain it, but even though she was so weak toward the end, her gratitude for the help I was giving her shined through it all. If you've ever helped someone like this, you know what I'm talking about. Those four months *in service to my good friend were a blessing to me, perhaps as much or more than they were to her.*

When it was all over, and Veronica's service had ended, I found out that she'd left me a note. Before she passed, she'd just paid off her house and had no one to leave it to. Now I'm no longer homeless; I'm living in the home, paid in full, that she gave to me.

By the simple act of helping another, we'll begin to feel better about ourself. It's a great truth that when we serve our friends and neighbors in need, we gain a new outlook on life, one that makes life worth living again. Our despair vanishes and is replaced by a joy that we may not have felt in a long time. Especially when we help someone who is worse off than we are, we will see the look of gratitude in their eyes as we're doing whatever we can to improve their circumstances. It may be bringing them a meal, or helping them get dressed, or brushing their hair, or even assisting them to be more comfortable in their last days on Earth. These small acts of love come back to us in ways we never imagined. For, in serving another, we are served. In loving another, we are loved. And in caring for another, we are cared for in such great measure that life itself takes on a profound, new direction. Once again, like little children who can't wait to go out and play with their friends after dinner, we rediscover the value and the preciousness of having a body and using it for all it's worth.

Mainstream Miscreation #1 ~ Health Issues
How We Create Illness
(and how we can transmute it.)

Have you ever wondered how all of our sicknesses and diseases came about? They were created by somebody, just like everything else in our world. *Ultimately, it is we who create our own sickness,* although quite often these maladies start out in someone else's mind, and we simply buy into their persuasive ideas.

When you think about it, humanity is very suggestible. We tend to think that since someone with supposed authority repeats the same idea over and over with power and fortitude that it must be true. But this, as more of us who are beginning to question these disease-laden ideas are discovering, is far from the reality we really want to be creating for ourselves.

Our sicknesses and diseases are sold to us like cars and trucks. They're *miscreated* in secret offices and hidden laboratories by people who are paid to think them up, people who do not care about the well-being of others in this world. Our challenge, as average, everyday citizens, is to learn to withhold our agreement from their sales promotions. When we're able to "just say no" and withstand the pressure of their pervasive sales methods, then we're more apt to remain happy and healthy. If, however, we're unable to withstand their persuasive techniques, and we buy into their sick ideas, then we set ourselves up for having to experience the very diseases they're selling.

Lately, when I've gone into a big box superstore, I've had to walk past a maze of advertising that proclaims, "Get your flu shot here today!" The signs are everywhere. You can't miss them. Then, while I'm standing in the checkout line, I can't help but overhear a conversation between the three people standing behind me. They're saying that it's flu season again, and it's looks like it's going to be worse than ever this year. I cringe at the thought of what they're creating for themselves.

Then, when I reach the checkout lady, she's wearing a big pink badge offering me another chance to deal with an even more dangerous disease. She rings me up and asks me if I'd like to contribute to "such and such foundation" for treating the illness on the badge she's wearing. I politely decline and go on my way.

By the time I got back to my car, I realized that I'd been confronted by three separate opportunities to manifest varying sicknesses—and if I were to believe in any one of them, I'd be running the risk of creating it in my own life. At the very least, by buying into any of these miscreations, I'd be reinforcing the overall collective belief in them. I'd be part of the problem, instead of the solution.

As pointed out earlier, the ultimate decision about who or what we believe always resides within us, in our thoughts. Do we want to believe the disease salespeople and take the chance of getting sick, or can we be strong and stand up for our own innate wellness? Per the *Law of Attraction*, which says that all of our experiences, including our wellness and sickness experiences, begin first in our mind, we always have the choice of what we want to think, and thus create for ourselves. And, at the same time, per the *Law of Agreement,* which says we have to live out that which we agree to, we always have the choice to agree with or withhold our agreement from any issues or beliefs that are presented to us. These options are important; they play a much greater role in our lives than we may know because they determine the quality of experiences we're going to have from then on.

Your thoughts and your future experiences
are directly related.
True or false?

Every time I see my friend, Keith, he has to tell me all about his liver challenges. Last weekend, we were grazing the salad bar at the local pub, and he told me that his doctor just downgraded his liver disease from stage 4 to stage 3. Already, it's too much information for me, especially at dinnertime.

In fact, I temporarily tune Keith out as I flash on the number of times I've talked to him about his habit of announcing the status of his disease to everyone. The Law of Attraction just hasn't registered yet, no matter how many times I've gone through it with him. He doesn't get that his thoughts and his words are adding to his illness, and that every time he talks about it, he's reinforcing his own health issue, an issue you'd think he'd rather not have to deal with. Who knows, his symptoms might go away entirely if he'd just stop telling everyone about them every chance he gets. He's yet to learn that some things in life are not for public consumption; they're only to be shared on a "need to know" basis, lest we make our challenges worse. I know the Highest Good is at work here, but it doesn't keep me from wondering if there's anything I could say or do that would help my good friend stop from reinforcing his own illness?

Everything returns to the basic premise that our thoughts and words are creating it all. Our tests in life always come back to asking ourselves: *Is what I'm thinking and talking about going to serve me and my friends? Is what I'm thinking and talking about going to provide me with the results and outcomes I'm intending for myself and others?* When we run these questions past our mind, who among us would *consciously* choose to experience sickness?

No one.

It's not in your Highest Good to suffer.
Suffering is not required.

Left alone to decide for oneself, every sane person would choose wellness—and there are at least two tried-and-true ways to bring that wellness into our life. First, we can learn to refrain from judging the sickness sellers, and we can *overlook* their sales tactics entirely. And second, we can see ourselves in our Highest Light and hold that vision, no matter what. When faced with the onslaught of the sickness sellers, we can remain steadfast and envision being happy, living in optimum health, and enjoying our life to the fullest. The Highest Light option is always available to us, and it's never farther than a thought away.

It's a strange custom in our culture to talk openly, even casually, about our friends who are sick. I was at a party recently standing next to a group of ladies who were gabbing about our mutual friend, Nicole, and her health issues. This was supposed to be a gathering of spiritually-minded people, so when I heard them mention a doctor's thoughtless diagnosis, I couldn't help but interrupt.

"You know," I said, "you're not helping Nicole by what you're chatting about. Thoughts are things, and they instantly cross the ethers and are received by the person you're discussing. This reinforces her illness, instead of her wellness. Is that what you really want to be doing for our friend?"

Well, it caught them off-guard at first, and they stopped talking just long enough for it to settle in. After a moment, one of them thanked me for the reminder, and the others nodded in agreement. Then they asked how they could be helping Nicole, and I said, "Why don't we all see her at her best, full of happiness, and in perfect health?"

In that instant, the whole tone of the conversation shifted, and we all felt better because we knew that we were doing something to help Nicole, rather than harming her.

When we *transmute* our health issues, we're rising above that which could affect us negatively, rendering it helpless in the face of our intent and determination. No longer are we subjected to unwanted experiences because, now, we've learned to change or *transmute* them. No longer will we be influenced into *miscreating* a situation that doesn't serve us or our fellow travelers. Instead, we look at every idea that comes our way and ask ourself whether it serves us or not. If it's something we really want to be creating, we can move toward it. If, on the other hand, our new viewpoint or belief doesn't seem like something we'd want to be manifesting, then we *transmute* it by simply *overlooking* it and maintaining a positive point of view. Unless we've been poisoned, it always helps to remember that we get sick because we're taught to get sick. We're programmed for it. We learn it from others. Germ theory is a good example. Most people believe that germs are the cause of our illnesses, neglecting to realize that our diseases, like everything else in our lives, begin in our thoughts. When we were very young, someone taught us that germs can make us sick. We believed them, and because of the *Law of Attraction,* we opened ourselves up to catching all sorts of maladies from others. Again, it's the thought of germs that makes us susceptible to their insidious manifestations.

I don't normally have houseguests, but last month I had a close friend come by. Patrick and I always enjoy visiting with each other, although on this visit he arrived with a persistent cough. Now I must tell you that in the old days, before I learned to mentally combat these issues, I would have been very concerned about "catching" his cough. On this occasion, however, I was able to welcome Patrick and invite him to stay as long as he liked because I've learned to handle these kinds of things differently.

Nowadays, I see these situations as opportunities to sharpen my vigilance at watching my thoughts. In fact, Patrick gave me many such opportunities over the course of his visit because every time he went through a heavy coughing spell, I'd always notice a nagging voice in my head, saying, "You could catch his cough. You know how contagious it is. Don't get too close to him," and on and on. And every time I would hear these ugly voices, without exception, I emphatically applied the opposite thought, telling myself, "Get behind me! I'm fine! I'm in perfect health!" and so forth. And you know what? It worked beautifully. Pat and I had a great week together, and as I write this, I'm in excellent health because I didn't listen to the nagging, sickness-producing voices that came into my mind. Instead, I stood up, steadfast and strong, for my own natural wellness.

Contagion is a belief we learned when we were very young, but now it's time for those of us who are beginning to understand that our thoughts create our future experiences to unlearn some of our old limited thinking habits and to stand firm for positive outcomes only. That's the way we *transmute* unwanted experiences and keep them from coming into our lives. We remain healthy by staying on the positive side of every belief that comes into our mind.

For as long as I can remember I've had to deal with blockages in my nasal passages. Recently, however, I was able to trace this issue back to a time when I was very young and had a runny nose from the cold, humid, Illinois winter. As I looked back to the source of my lifelong nasal issues, I saw a time when my mother and I were standing in front of the sink in our small kitchen. She was wiping my nose with a hand towel and telling me I had "sinus troubles."

I must not have been over two or three years old because I was just learning to recognize certain words at that point in my life. Certainly, I didn't know that my mother was programming me to have "sinus troubles" from then on. I wasn't old enough to realize that she was a registered nurse and looked at life through the eyes of a medical practitioner who had names (like "sinus troubles") and diagnoses for every symptom in the book. Instinctively, I trusted her to take good care of me.

As a result, I believed her and created "sinus troubles" for myself until they became a normal occurrence on and off throughout the whole of my life. I had no idea that my thoughts were creating my future back then.

Fast forward to the present. Nowadays I don't suffer from "sinus troubles" like I used to because I've cleared this issue by tracing it back to its source, back to that time with my mother in the kitchen. I've remembered that my thoughts are creating my physical circumstances, and I've reprogrammed my body to follow my mind's instructions. So, when I went back there in my mind, I told my mom the exact opposite of her "sinus troubles" diagnosis, which was that "I'm fine!" Then, I intended, for the Highest Good, that my sinus passages are clear now and forevermore.

Of course, like all lifelong habits, the thought of nasal congestion still occasionally pops up. But when it does, I overlook it entirely and put my attention elsewhere. I take a deep breath through my perfectly clear nose, and I tell myself, "I'm fine!"

We Intenders *transmute* all unserving beliefs by *overlooking* them entirely, keeping 100% focused only on positive outcomes, and not allowing even a single naysaying shred of doubt to touch upon our consciousness. *While other people are believing in and creating unwanted experiences for themselves, we choose to keep our thoughts in a positive vein by telling ourselves the opposite.* In this way, whenever we're introduced to an obvious *miscreation* (getting sick, hard times, enemies on our doorstep, etc.), we immediately think the appropriate opposite thought. For instance, we can tell ourself, *"I'm in excellent health, I am victorious, I am abundant, I'm vibrating at a very high level, I am totally safe."* In other words, we never move off of our positive stance. We never give a name to any disease, and we never buy into sickness in any form. Since our thoughts are creating our future physical reality, it simply doesn't serve us to entertain thoughts of ill health.

There is much controversy about people wanting to leave the Earth these days. Many seem to think that life is so bad here that they need to find a way out. However, that viewpoint doesn't serve you. The decision to leave should not be about running away because of the harsh conditions here at this time; it should be more about weighing the pros and cons of staying or going.

If you stay, you'll remain tethered to a body that's tethered to the Earth, but you'll still have the opportunity to overcome your challenges and find the joy that lies behind them. If you leave, however, you'll lose the opportunity to finish what you came here to do. You'll lose the opportunity to fulfill your soul's reason for being here, and you will likely have to come back and take up where you left off.

The thoughtforms surrounding you that suggest you should leave this Earth because it's hard or harsh here are deceiving you. You're experiencing these hard, harsh conditions, not because it's a bad place to be, for it is truly a precious gift to be living on the Earth at this point in time. You're experiencing harshness because you've forgotten about your purpose here, which is to Love. Once you remember to let go of judging everything around you and begin to Love it all, the Highest Good will rally to your side and support you in all that you do.

Lee Ching

43

Oftentimes people just roll over and accept their dying.
People need to keep going
when the doctor gives them a death sentence.
They need to keep moving forward.
They need to think about their purpose for being here,
instead of just doing what they're told to do.

{Remember}
The Earth Is Beautiful

Our Earth is a place of such awesome beauty that we never want to take it for granted. As it happens, however, the hustle-bustle of the world today often distracts us from appreciating the beauty that surrounds us. We tend to get so involved in the business matters of life that we neglect to get away from them on a regular basis and digest our worldly experiences, much in the same way that we would digest a good meal. One of the best ways to renew ourself when we've become overloaded at work is to take a walk out in nature. There we will find our freedom from all the cares and concerns of the workaday world. There we will be renewed.

When was the last time you took a drive out past the edge of town, got out of your car, and started walking? If it's been a while, you're overdue. For within a few steps, as the trees and rocks begin to close in around you, you'll notice a difference in the way you feel. The air seems lighter; the sky seems bluer; the world seems to breathe a sigh of relief, and bids you to walk further. Whether you follow the trail or leave it behind, suddenly small things you may not have otherwise noticed reveal themselves: the depth of color in a fallen leaf; the wind's rustling through the branches; the chipmunk peeking out at you from behind a rock.

You breathe even deeper now as you lengthen your stride. In a clearing, you stop and feel as if the ancients may have visited this area centuries ago, enthralled by its beauty. By a small stream, you feel the flow of life calling you to let go and see where it takes you. Coming to an opening in the forest, you feel the majesty of the mountains in the distance, and you feel as if Mother Earth herself, in all her radiant beauty, is welcoming you and cradling you in her loving embrace.

The Earth is a living Being
and she responds to you
as you respond to her.

Take time to get away. Take time to go to the water and put your feet in it. Mother Earth will ground you and take all your pent-up energy and suck it right out of the bottom of your feet into the cool water. Take time to drive far from the city and out into the desert or the remote countryside where you'll feel an expansion in your soul. Go to where there is nothing manmade around you, and this expansion will relieve you of all you left behind. Breathe deep of the Earth's beauty wherever you go, for it is everywhere.

If you're unable to get away, get yourself some houseplants or a loving pet. Just having a few houseplants around you has a way of calming and bringing peace into your life. Or, pet a kitten and soak up the love that comes through her purr. Play with a dog and sense the loyal friendship he offers you. The animals are there to help and heal us. In quiet moments, we can even become One with them.

These things are all manifestations of the Earth's beauty. Immerse yourself in it until you're filled to the brim. Then, when you're ready, give Mother Earth your thanks and return to your daily life refreshed and renewed. Who knows? Maybe you'll decide to spend more time out in the country. Maybe you'll even decide to live there.

Caring about life is for our Highest Good. If we didn't care about life, we wouldn't be here to fulfill our purpose on this Earth. For caring about life—all life— comes from our soul. It's something we're born with. I live in a small southern Colorado town at 7200 feet in the Rockies. Yesterday, I was driving to the recycling center with my stuff and enjoying the view of the last snowmelt on the surrounding peaks. The road to the center winds through a couple of miles of pine forest, and as I rounded a bend, there, crossing the road right in front of me, was a family of about a dozen deer. No other cars were coming from either direction, so I pulled over just to take in this amazing sight.

The deer were all ages and sizes, from the huge older buck and his gorgeous doe, to the new spring babies. As you may know, deer are completely oblivious to cars and roadways, and they can take their sweet time ambling across the road—which was nice for me because I was able to sit there, not ten feet away, and watch them for several minutes.

As the last of the herd was heading into the trees on the other side of the road, one teenage doe stopped right beside my car and stared at me with those gentle, innocent, curious eyes. Her ears, which at that age seemed to have grown twice as fast as the rest of her body, stood straight up, listening intently. In that moment, it was only me and her, looking at each other. I don't know what she was thinking, but, for me, those few moments were a true gift.

When she passed by and went into the pines to catch up with her family, I remember, as I drove on, feeling like this was my lucky day. She was as beautiful as anything I'd ever seen.

Caring is your calling.
The more you care,
the more you're cared for.

How would our world look if all of us were to honor the Highest Good for all our earthly creatures, including ourselves? *Can you imagine it?* First and foremost, we'd begin to respect the lifestyles of other people. We'd immediately stop interfering in the lives of our fellowmen and women and let them pursue, without interruption, what they came here to do. Just this one small change in our behavior would bring rewards beyond measure. As personal gain goes by the wayside in favor of the Highest Good for all, those who've been encumbered and enslaved would begin to seek out their purpose in life and open up to new avenues previously thought to be unattainable. The poor and downtrodden, and even the average Joe and Jill, who previously had to watch out for their unruly neighbors, would now be able to live freer, more comfortable lives. The humble man and woman, who want only to live quietly in peace, would be able to do so. Indeed, anyone who wanted to pursue personal happiness and the refined inner qualities of life would be left alone to do so now that the Highest Good of everyone is being respected.

Once people have found peace within themselves, they would come together to create clean, supportive environments that serve everyone's best interests. *Can you imagine it?* All pollution is gone, replaced by a newfound intent to keep our Mother Earth pristine. Money based economies are gone, replaced by intelligent, resource-based systems. Zero-point energy, providing free energy for everyone, has replaced unclean gas, oil, coal, and nuclear grids. Our Mother Earth shines like never before, now that her original integrity and beauty have returned for all to enjoy.

And finally, our entire culture blossoms. Everywhere you look, you see smiles on the faces of everyone around you. You see the light of excitement and enthusiasm in the glowing of their eyes. The human spirit has entered the hearts and minds of all people now that we're honoring all life and doing what we came here to do. Now, all of us, en masse, are truly reborn, not just in word, but in deed. Now, God and all Her loving angels reveal themselves and shower us with Grace and Divine Love ... and that's just the beginning...

Can you imagine it? It's all within our reach. And all we have to do is intend it, and line our intentions up with the Highest Good.

You have known before you came here
that there would be a time
when you would be called upon.
The time which you have been awaiting has come.
It's time for you to align with the Highest Good,
and to care for all of life in every moment.

{Remember}
We're Meant to Play

Playtime is the great re-energizer. Whenever we're feeling stagnant and need a boost, we can go out and play, and everything will get better for us. It doesn't matter what sport or form it takes; it could be pitching horseshoes, swimming at the pool, or running around the neighborhood. It could be playing basketball, golf, skiing down the slopes, or walking briskly through the local park. Even when we aren't able work out or exercise, we can go play cards, or scrabble, or bingo with friends. What matters is that we do what we really like to do.

We can play alone or with a team. In fact, playing with friends seems to double the enjoyment we get from it. Remember when you were growing up and you played with the neighborhood kids after school? Wasn't that one of the best times in your life? Then, somewhere along the way, life took on a more serious tone, and you found that you didn't have as much time to go out and play. You set your playtime aside in favor of more important things.

Life went on and your body began to remind you for the need to recreate itself, and you paid a price, physically, if you didn't listen to it. If, however, you did listen, and you left your work and went out and played, you found that playing is an instinctive thing. You discovered that your body needs to be turned loose periodically, without your thinking getting in the way.

Indeed, our instincts call upon us to give our thoughts a break every-so-often so our body can take over for a while. For it's in our body's "taking over" that we become more alert, more agile, more aware of what's going on around us. Relying solely on our instincts, a message is sent to our body that we trust it to do its best on our behalf, and that's when it gets really fun! The rest of the world goes away, as we let go and play with wild abandon. Then, when we're done playing, tired, and ready to go back to our normal routines, we'll notice a wonderful side effect to our having gone out and played. Not only is our physical body strengthened and more supple, our Spirit is quickened. We feel better able to take on whatever is next in our life. We feel refreshed and ready for anything.

So, the next time you're feeling a bit overwhelmed by life and you need some downtime, go out and play. Put everything else that's been weighing you down on hold for a while, go have fun, and give it all you've got until you're completely saturated. That's when playing is at its best: when you've totally immersed yourself in it, caring only about the moment. Then, after you're finished and headed to the showers, even though your body may be sweaty and sore, notice how happy your Spirit is. Chances are you won't want to wait so long before you decide to go out and play again.

Think – if you could be doing
what makes you the most happy.
Then go and do it.

We're Meant to Be Happy

Most people want to feel good. We want our lives to run smoothly. We want friends and happy experiences. Why, then, would we ever want to sabotage ourselves from having good things happen by harboring contradictory thoughts? "We wouldn't," you say. But after thinking about it, you add, "But we do!" This is the crux of one of life's most puzzling paradoxes: we want happiness, but we think thoughts that will never get us there. Unconsciously, all sorts of thoughts are rambling through our heads all day long and, although these thoughts are working their way outward into our daily interactions, we rarely bother to tame or *overlook* the ones that aren't serving us. And we rarely decide to concentrate on the ones that will give us what we truly want.

For years I didn't understand why all these weird experiences kept coming my way. It was usually little things, frustrating things. I'd have car trouble when I was running late; I'd go shopping for items I needed, and they'd be out of them; I'd go out on blind dates that wouldn't work out. It seemed like it was one thing after another. My entire life felt like it was destined to create problems for itself.

Then, one evening I went to an Intenders Circle and our hostess, Diane, was explaining that it's wise to watch our thoughts. In her introduction to newcomers (like me), she said that we're all living under the Law of Attraction—she also called it the Intention Process —and that the people who are the happiest are the ones who get what they want, while attracting less of what they don't want.

According to her, the Law works like this: Everything we're thinking has the potential to work its way into our daily life; it just depends on how much attention we put on it. The more we keep our attention on a thought, the more it's apt to manifest. "This is important," she said, "because it explains why some people keep drawing unwanted, adverse events into their lives. It's because they're holding their thoughts on undesirable experiences; they're doubting or worrying, both of which tend to bring them the exact opposite of what they really want."

"When we're doubting or worrying," she said, "we're envisioning things going wrong ... and so they do! That's when we need to 'change the channel', like

we would on the TV when the program we're watching isn't enjoyable anymore. We simply stop thinking about what we don't want, and switch to thinking about what we do want. Then everything gets better for us."

She went on for another few minutes expanding on the Law to make sure we understood what she was saying, then she told us about the Highest Good. She said that it would keep us from having so many undesirable things happen to us. Even if we caught ourself mulling repetitive, unserving thoughts over in our mind, the Highest Good would override these doubts and worries and make sure we began drawing better experiences into our life.

Well, the little talk Diane shared with us that night changed everything for me. Now I understood how my thoughts were affecting my daily life. It made me pay more attention to what I was thinking and manifesting for myself. That Intenders Circle was just under a year ago and, since then, I've been watching my thoughts more closely, and I "change the channel" whenever I notice that I'm doubting or worrying—and you know what? No more car problems. No more fruitless trips to the store. No more strange blind dates because I met the man of my dreams! Now with the Highest Good at work in my life, I'm not attracting those frustrating situations like I used to. Thanks to my new friend, Diane, and the Intenders, I'm enjoying my life like never before.

Linda Poznanski

> **Think about what you do want,**
> **and don't think about what you don't want.**

Changes are happening constantly in our physical world. Nothing is permanent. It's all in motion. One minute we could be on top of the world in the most pleasurable state imaginable, and soon after that we may have to deal with pain and suffering we never saw coming. The critical point here, as we pursue our happiness, is to find a way to handle our changes gracefully.

When we seek to deal with the ups and downs in our physical world, our emotions come into play. By learning to retain a more positive outlook, no matter what's going on around us, we will live a happier life. Conversely, when we get fearful or mad at every little change, letting our negative emotions run amuck, we harm ourselves, often in ways we don't see. Our negative reactions to life's changing situations affect our immune system, our overall health, our relationships, our decision-making, and our entire outlook on life. The more we turn our negativity loose by being angry or sorrowful, the more we invite suffering into our life. From this point of view, we waste our precious energy, energy we could be using for higher purposes.

Life's lessons typically involve energy management, with anger being one of our greatest challenges. When we're angry, it's like we have leaks, similar to carrying around a bucket of water that has a hole in it. By the time we get to the place where we want to use the water (for the hissing car radiator, or the thirsty plants across the yard), the water is half gone, and we'll have to make another trip. It's the same in our lives. If all our emotional energy is leaked out in the form of anger or irritability, we won't have enough to bring it up from our solar plexus into our heart area where the most profound of experiences awaits us.

However, once we're able to hold our negative emotions in check, and we build them up by not reacting to all of the changes going on around and within us, we'll have enough energy for our Spirit to shine.

My dad had a temper like no one I ever met. He'd fly off the handle at the smallest thing, and (like father, like son), he passed his temper along to me. In fact, his father and his father before him—going back through my entire ancestral line for generations—had issues with their tempers that we, and our loved ones, had to deal with.

It wasn't until one of our early Intenders spiritual guidance sessions that I asked Lee Ching about my anger issues, and he told me that intolerance and irritability had tormented my ancestors for generations, and that I was the last in a long line of relatives who struggled with their negativity. Then I asked him why and where this irritability originally started, and his reply was an eye-opener. He said that, in times past, humanity did not enjoy all the comforts and conveniences we take for granted today. He said that my ancestors had had to experience the whole gamut of horrific situations: everything from tortures and imprisonment to daily hunger and starvation. Oftentimes there was little or no food, no shelter from the cold, no safe haven from vicious marauders, much less from the lords and governors who taxed us beyond our ability to pay. Life was harsh and lawless, and my ancestors' anger developed over lifetimes out of those harsh conditions.

When I asked Lee Ching how to counteract my angry temperament, he said, "As you spend more time in quiet meditation, Tony, instead of constantly stimulating yourself with all the pleasures and treasures of this life, over time you'll come to a place of peace within yourself. The more you can cultivate stillness within your mind, as well as in your negative emotions, the sooner you'll begin to calm down, like the ocean waves that become smooth and still after a raging storm."

I was lost in thought and so was everyone else in the circle. They knew Lee Ching's words pertained to them as well as to me. After a short pause, he went on to say, "Anyone who has practiced meditation for any length of time will tell you that it's cumulative; that it just gets better and better. If you want to be able to stay centered and balanced, regardless of whatever's going on around you, recreate yourself every single day through meditation and being out in nature."

These are two great ways to better manage our emotional energy: We calm our hearts and minds through daily meditation, and we take regular walks in the trees, and parks, and along the shorelines. By meditating and getting out in nature, we become calmer and less apt to explode in anger at every little thing. At the same time, we'll be storing up our emotional energy so it can be used for other things, like producing our creative projects, or having a higher inner experience. You see, these emotional energies can be rerouted so that, instead of spilling them out, we can use them to further our inner growth.

Whenever I'm angry or frustrated, my Course in Miracles friend, Jason, reminds me that my emotional upset is always another opportunity for me to forgive. Forgiveness, he says, is another way, along with meditation and being in nature, of dealing with our anger issues.

When I told Jason that I recently had my computer break down at a critical point in my work—and that I didn't get mad and yell at the world, like I used to—he said that I was consciously taking advantage of another opportunity to forgive. He pointed out that, like a lot of people, I'd been blaming or judging the world for my adversity, thinking that the world is out to get me.

But lately, since I've started watching my thoughts and actions more closely, he says that I'm utilizing challenging situations, like my crashed computer, as another opportunity to forgive whoever or whatever I'd been blaming or judging for my problems. In this way, whenever I remember to practice forgiveness, I'm no longer giving into my lifelong tendency to react emotionally toward every crazy situation that comes up in my life. Instead, I've realized that the world isn't really out to get me, and I'm staying aligned with the Highest Good by remaining calmer and more collected in the midst of life's constant changes.

Michael Knapp

In order to get the handle on our negative emotions, life becomes a regular balancing act. We want to store up enough emotional energy for higher purposes, and, at the same time, we don't want to become so overloaded with fear and emotional charge that we're unable to manage it without causing problems for ourself and others. You see, when we're filled with more emotional charge than we're accustomed to holding, we often tend to explode it outward onto our family, friends, and loved ones—and this is precisely what we want to avoid. Why? Because it causes backlashes and comes back to us in ways we generally don't like. When we're feeling overloaded with charge, or feeling like we're ready to react harshly, we need to find a way to let go of the charge without dumping it on our fellow travelers. Scream it into a pillow, or go out into the woods where nobody is around, and let 'er rip. In this way, we drain out any excess emotional energies that we're unable to handle, and, at the same time, we're diffusing any potentially ugly situations with our loved ones that we would wish, later on, we wouldn't have created.

It's never a good idea to dump your excess emotional baggage on a friend.

Mainstream Miscreation #2
Unbalanced Emotions
How We Create Fear
(and how we can transmute it.)

I live on the edge of town where people sometimes bring their unwanted animals and drop them off to survive on their own. Last year, a couple of young, orange tabby cats showed up in my yard. They appeared to be brothers, and, right away, I could tell that they didn't get along very well together. What with their constant hissing and fighting over what little food they could come up with, I had to break them apart more than once. Feral and wild, they survived by hanging around my place, catching mice and small birds.

Somewhere in the middle of last year's harsh winter, the larger, more aggressive of the two cats died in the heavy snow, leaving the smaller, sweeter one to go it alone. Now, with the coming year's snows on the way, I'm feeding Red Kitty—that's what I call him—because I'm concerned he might not make it through the cold Colorado nights over the next four months. Although he shows up by the back door every morning and evening to receive a bowl of crunchies and whatever else I can find to feed him, he won't come into the house, even though the cat door is always open. If I could just get him to come in for the winter, he'd survive nicely in the warmth of the house. He's so timid and fearful, however, that every time I get close to him, he immediately bolts across the yard and is gone. His fear is keeping him from enjoying the comforts of a warm home and, at the same time, it's threatening his *life because he runs the risk of freezing overnight out in the relentless cold.*

Red Kitty reminds me of "we the people" in so many ways. We could easily be comfortable and happy if we would just let go of our fears. As it stands now, we tend to take all of the constant, mainstream scare-stories to heart and give into our fears on a moment to moment basis. I don't know about you, but I've had enough of all the fear going around. It's like I'm having to look over my shoulder all the time. If a bill isn't paid by the due date, I risk being fined. If I don't pay those exorbitant taxes, I go to jail. If I happen to be going two miles over the speed limit, it's my fear, not my inclination to drive safer, that slows me down. If I don't conform and comply with all these things (and many more), I'll stand out and take the chance of losing what little freedom I do have.

Red Kitty runs away because he's afraid; he doesn't realize how good it could be if he would gather his courage, overcome his fears, and come in from the snow. It's the same with us. It's like we're mesmerized by a system that's keeping us from reaching our highest, happiest potential, not realizing things don't have to stay the way they are. If we would imagine what it can be like when we're not having to conform to every law and cultural value, we would begin to create comfort for ourselves. We could stop looking over our shoulders. Our fears would lessen, and our Highest Good would take over.

For the time being, we may not yet be able to stop paying our debts and taxes, but we can envision what it would be like if we were 100% free; we can imagine how good it feels once we're totally and finally unencumbered. When we put our attention on that good feeling, and on that vision of freedom, someday, in the not-too-distant future, our visions will come to life, and we will, at last, be free.

Life on Earth doesn't have to be hard and uncompromising. We make it that way because we don't see the possibilities available to us. We don't see that we could live very comfortably without having a lot of legal encumbrances and financial obligations. They're unnecessary and we can easily do without them, and the fears that go along with them. I hear Red Kitty at the back door now. I'll keep you posted on his status but, in the meantime, know that he's getting more than enough food to keep him alive and full-bellied for the winter. He's such a sweet little guy. I intend that he comes inside . . .

Life is an amazing gift.
We have to experience it,
not run away from it.

Fear is the opposite of feeling good and being happy. One could almost say that fear makes our mainstream world go around. Everywhere we look nowadays people are steeped in fear. Our reactions to life's changes are typically fearful; we're afraid something bad will happen. And because that's what we're putting our attention on, that's what we can expect to happen down the road. That's the first lesson in fear: the more we hold onto a frightening thought, the more we can expect to have to deal with it in real life.

So, how do we keep these fears from manifesting in our lives? To begin with, we must become more vigilant of our thinking processes and realize that our thoughts are flying through our mind at breakneck speed. They're moving much faster than our earthly hands and feet. We need *a quickening in our awareness* if we're going to keep our fears from coming to the surface of our lives. We need to notice them right away, nip them in the bud, and turn our attention to something

67

more positive before our fears gain the least bit of momentum. If we don't catch them right away, they have a way of staying with us, sometimes for days, or weeks, or lifetimes.

Most of my life has been riddled with fear, and understandably so. My mother was more afraid of life than anyone I ever knew. Whenever I tried to freely express myself, she'd invariably say something like, "Tony, don't do that or else you'll hurt yourself." Or, "Tony, stop it or I'll call your dad, and he'll take the strap to you."

I always had to watch out for everything, and as I grew older and left home, the world had no problem replacing my mother's threats with threats of its own. No matter where I turned, if I did the "wrong thing", I'd be in trouble. It seemed like there was always something bad that could happen.

It wasn't until I met a man with no apparent fear that I began to figure out how my fears worked, and how to deal with them. I remember one occasion when BJ and I were clearing an area in the dense Kona rainforest and talking about fear as we worked. We had a crazy neighbor, Doug, who was as mean as a snake and was always threatening everybody who lived along our country road. I was especially upset about it, and no longer felt safe working on my own land for fear that Doug would come through the bushes at any time and beat me up.

"If you keep dwelling on people coming through the bushes and attacking you," BJ said, "that's what will happen sooner or later. Is that what you really want?"

"No!" I answered emphatically. "Obviously, I want to work around here in peace, without having to look over my shoulder every time the wind rattles through the palm fronds."

"Then you'll need to find a way to keep your peace, and that involves you paying much closer attention to the thoughts that are running through your head."

"But BJ," I said, "my thoughts are moving so fast. How will I ever notice them all?"

He put down his machete, stopped working, and faced me. "You have to start somewhere," he said. "This may sound a little strange to you, but your thoughts have weight. Some thoughts are heavier, and they tend to take up more of your attention than others. These are the thoughts that are easiest to start with in your efforts to free yourself from your fears because they don't fly by as fast. With practice, you'll learn to catch the lighter, faster ones too, but, in the meantime, it's best to start by taking notice of the heavier, more repetitive thoughts, the ones you keep constantly mulling over—even though you know they're not for your Highest Good."

"Thoughts have different weights?" I said. "This is all new to me."

BJ went on, "While you're working around the land, in your mind, you keep seeing crazy Doug come through the bushes at you. That thought keeps recurring. It has a lot of weight, doesn't it?"

"I guess so."

"Well, that gives you the perfect opportunity to learn how to stop that repetitious, fearful thought from continuing to haunt you. Here's what you do: the next time you're working, and you notice the thought of crazy Doug, or a wild boar, or anything else coming through the bushes at you, you immediately look around and bring your attention back to the present moment, back to the here and now. Just let that thought go, and put your attention back on the work at hand."

"Then what do I do if the fear thought comes back again right away?"

"At first, it will," he said. "But with vigilance and increased awareness, you'll be able to notice those

70

fearful thoughts much quicker than you did before. Then you can immediately turn your attention elsewhere. The longer you hold onto the repetitive fear thoughts, the longer they'll hang on. On the other hand, the quicker you catch the fearful thoughts, and turn your attention onto something else—either on a more positive, uplifting thought, or on whatever is in front of you at the time—the quicker you'll be free of your fears and their incumbent manifestations."

From that day forward, I began watching my thoughts a lot closer, and whenever any thought that I wouldn't want to be manifesting arose in my mind, I immediately switched my attention to something else. Sometimes I'd switch it to another thought that led to a more positive outcome, and sometimes I'd switch it to paying closer attention to what I was working on at the time. In either case, the thoughts of fear seemed to bother me less and less over time, and my life became happier because I was getting free from my fears.

**What you are looking to create
is a positive, happy life for yourself—
and the more you intend
that your thoughts are positive and happy,
the more that is what you will create.**

71

Everything Is All Right
If We Believe It Is

Clearing is a process of ridding ourselves of our fearful emotional baggage and knee-jerk reactions by searching our mind back to where someone taught us that things were "wrong." In other words, we locate the origin of our guilt, so we can bring it to light, acknowledge it, turn it around, and let it go. In this way, we effectively dissolve our ego, so our Spirit can shine through.

Any bona-fide clearing process requires a strong measure of permission. Before helping another person dissolve their ego and their conditioned hang-ups, the teacher must always have the student's permission or agreement to do so. In my case, when BJ told me that he'd be willing to push my buttons and help me get clear, he explained the process thoroughly, and then asked me, "Is it alright with you if I assist you in your clearing by showing you some of your triggers? We'll be doing this for the purpose of helping you become free and clear from your emotional reactions, so you can begin to transmute some of the things that are unconsciously holding you back from reaching your highest potential."

Of course, I agreed—and right away BJ began showing me my unconscious tendencies to label people, places, and things as "not alright." By pushing my buttons, he was bringing all the things I thought weren't alright in my life to light. Without exception, his button-pushing would flash me back to a time and place where I'd learned that something wasn't alright. My parents, schoolteachers, the TV, as well as my peers and friends, had taught me that something was "wrong", and I'd bought into it.

Then, after isolating a past, judgmental experience, I'd clear it out by telling myself that it was alright. For instance, I used to think it wasn't alright to be as reclusive as I am. I felt guilty for spending so much of my time alone. When I traced this issue back to its source by asking myself, "What's not alright with me being a hermit," I discovered a previous experience where my father had belittled me for wanting to stay in my room and read, when he wanted me to go out and caddy for him on the golf course. Going back to that incident in my mind, I told my dad that it's alright for me to be alone if I choose—and in that instant, my guilt started melting away. Now I enjoy my time alone, guilt-free.

The outcome of doing this exercise, according to BJ, would eventually take me to a place where everything is alright, and nothing is wrong in my life. I'd be clear.

As you can imagine, there were times when he'd trigger an old emotional response in me, and I'd get mad, "How can you say that to me?" I'd yell at him. "How can you treat me like this?" And his answer was always the same, "You gave me your permission," he'd say. "You wanted freedom from your triggers. You wanted to know what life is like without all your anger and judgments."

It was true. I wanted clear of my reactions, but at the time I had no idea what I was getting myself into. I must have been crazy! I'd given a friend access to my innermost personality in hopes of freeing myself from my reactive behavior. It wasn't until years later that I was able to thank BJ for showing me my buttons. In the long run, I was glad I'd given him my permission.

**When you're triggered,
where did you get those reactions?
Where did they come from?**

74

As we've said, right and wrong are judgments. They're only happening in our mind. By the same token, everything is all right if we choose it to be, and nothing is wrong unless we choose it to be. Once we understand this, there's nothing anyone can say to us that we're apt to take personally. We won't have any buttons others can push that trigger a reaction in us because everything is all right with us. The challenge with this is that most of us were taught at an early age to believe that we've sinned, and that things are wrong in this world—and especially that things are wrong with us. If, however, we *transcend* our "wrongness" and make everything all right, no matter what anyone says, then we'll be free from taking things so personally.

Clearing ourselves can happen in many different ways. Another avenue for getting clear opens up for us when we know that we're all things; when we understand that *we're whole*, and that, in our mind, there isn't anything we aren't, or can't be. When we acknowledge the parts of ourself that we wouldn't normally look at, and *we become them*, we get clear on another level altogether.

75

Some mystery schools are masters at showing you your buttons. They'll set up a situation, long before you set foot on their doorstep, whereby you come face-to-face with parts of yourself you wouldn't normally notice. In other words, you're a "mark" walking into a set-up. My first experience with one of these schools came when BJ and his friend, Nick, took me to one of their social gatherings. They were having fun, singing and playing music—and I'd brought my guitar along (because BJ suggested it), even though I was just learning how to play it in those days. As the evening went on, there was a lull in the music, and Nick said, "Hey, Tony, why don't you play us a song?"

Well, it caught me off-guard because he'd singled me out in front of the whole group. Somewhat reluctantly, I started into an old Beatles tune, and before I'd gotten halfway through the first verse, Nick went "Awww, man!" in a loud, derogatory voice.

*I felt horrible and stopped playing immediately. Then, to make matters worse, BJ picked up his guitar and launched into another Beatles tune: **Nowhere Man** —and if I could have disappeared into the woodwork, I gladly would have. They'd set me up in order to trigger a response from me that was supposed to show me how easily I tended to take things personally. At* the time, though, I was too frustrated to process what was really going on.

It wasn't until a few days later that BJ came by my little coffee shack for a visit. Fortunately, by that time I'd cooled off enough to be able to look back on it all more objectively. He explained that I was "marked" that night at the gathering, and he went on to elaborate. "If you want to be happy and free in this life, Tony," he said, "you'll need to become all of it. Not only will you need to be the hero and the good guy—in your mind—but you'll also have to learn to admit to being a fool or a failure. That's what Nick was trying to show you at the party ... that you react whenever someone makes fun of you or degrades you. But if you could have overlooked his deliberate rudeness and remained centered and happy with no reaction on your part, then no one could "get your goat", so to speak. You'd be free from your buttons."

"But how, exactly, do I do that, BJ?" I'm reacting to all sorts of triggers. Jeez, you can play a few bars of **Nowhere Man** and I get pissy!"

He laughed so hard I thought he was going to hurt himself. When he regained his composure, he said, "I repeat: you have to become all of it, Tony. In your mind, you have to have it be all right if you're the **Nowhere**

77

Man. *It has to be okay with you if someone calls you a fool, or a crazy person, or a jerk, or a failure, or worse—and the easiest way to do this is to admit to yourself to being a fool or a freak—because, in your mind, you're already all of these things."*

"I still don't get it," I said, in obvious confusion. "Why would I ever want to deliberately go out and be a fool or a failure?"

He chuckled again, then turned more serious, "We're not talking about what you're doing out in the world. We're only talking about what's going on inside your head. When you look closely, you'll see that you've been taught to take things personally, and I'm telling you that the opposite thought is evoked, as well as the one that strokes you. You can't have the hero without subtly bringing forth it's opposite, which is the fool. You can't be a success without evoking failure. So you might as well cop to being both the good guy and the bad guy because, in your mind, you are both of them. You're all of it ..."

He stopped talking, seeing that I needed a minute to let that settle in. "It's simple." he then went on. "You like being stroked, don't you, Tony?"

"Of course, BJ. Who doesn't like being praised?

It makes me feel good."

"I'm sure it does, but at the same time, just as soon as someone insults you, you go to pieces. I remind you that for every point of view you're holding onto —including every view you maintain and hold sacred about yourself—its opposite is just as valid. As it stands now, you're not acknowledging large parts of yourself that cause you to react in disagreement. But, what if you were able to keep your emotional kneejerk reactions in check? What if someone is calling you every name in the book, and you're able to remain calm and unaffected inside yourself?"

"I'd be happier. I'd be free. But, again, how do I do it?"

"Like I said, in your head, you cop to being all of it: the fool as well the hero, the shadow as well as the savior. In truth, that's what you already are. In your mind, you can be anyone or anything you choose. There isn't anything you can't think about yourself, but you keep limiting your thoughts to the favorable ones only. As soon as you're able to integrate the unfavorable ones—those where other people or the voices inside your head are calling you ugly names—the sooner you'll be free from your buttons."

"Integrate?"

"Yes, integrate, not eliminate!" he said. "If you continue to stuff the shadowy parts of yourself under the rug, avoiding them instead of copping to them, you'll never be free. But as soon as you realize, inside the sanctity of your own mind, that you're all of it, everything will come into focus for you." BJ paused for a moment, thinking, then continued. "You're all things, Tony, including all those nasty names people are apt to call you. When you stop limiting your thinking, you'll find that you have access to all thoughts, not just the ones that keep your ego propped up."

"But, BJ, what about my self esteem?" I asked. "How do I keep my confidence intact if I'm going to integrate the fool or the failure in me?"

"Believe me, Tony, your confidence is not in jeopardy. By knowing, inside yourself, that you're all things—the good, the bad, and the ugly, like in the Clint Eastwood movie—you'll begin to balance out all the thoughts about who you think you are. Eventually, you'll come to the point where you don't buy into any of those labels or boxes that others would like to put you in. You won't buy into whether you're right or wrong, good or bad, success or failure, hero or fool. You just are. You're a witness to it all, unaffected by *any of it — and you'll be treating the world and all of it's criticisms and insults like a passing parade that you're watching from a higher place, a place of freedom, a place of peace."*

"Sounds heavenly, BJ." I said.

"It is, Tony. That's when you'll find your true happiness ... when no matter what anyone says about you, you retain your inner joy and freedom. Isn't that what you really want for yourself?"

In order to have it all,
you have to be it all.

{Remember}
Good Friends Are Better Than Gold

Until we're permanently aware of what we're creating with our everyday thoughts and words, we need the help of our friends, especially when we catch ourself saying something we wouldn't really want to bring into manifestation. That's why it's good to hang out with like-minded and light-hearted people who will gently nudge us when we say something that's not going to give us the outcomes we're looking for. It happens all the time in our Intenders work, and we often ask our friends an extremely important question that we've consciously put in place to help us line up with the Highest Good. This question is: *Is what you're putting your attention on—in your thoughts and with your words—going to give you the results you're looking for?*

**Whatever you're talking about—
whether it's positive or negative,
something you want
or something you don't want—
is on its way to you.**

I have a lady friend, Naomi, who comes to our circles and is typically down in the dumps. Every time we see her, she has to tell us about all the things going wrong in her life. Either she's been sick, or broke, or lonely. You name it. It's like she's constantly maintaining a vested interest in her negative thoughts; they're soothing her in some perverse way. Since we're good friends, I casually mentioned her habitual behavior to her one evening when she seemed more receptive than usual.

"Naomi, don't you realize that by complaining about your situation all the time, you're perpetuating it; that just by continuing to dwell on these things that are troubling you, you're creating the perfect environment for them to keep returning?" I asked.

"I'm not sure what you're talking about, Tony. What do you mean?"

"I'm saying that your thoughts and your words are the forerunners of your experiences. If you keep telling everyone about all your problems, then your problems will continue to make trouble for you."

"What am I supposed to do, then?" she asked, sincerely. "If I don't tell anyone about my problems, they won't be able to help me!"

I thought about this. Clearly, she didn't understand that the Highest Good would help her, if she would only change her thinking and speaking habits. "You don't trust that your thoughts and words are creating your future," I said to her. "If you could learn to think and speak in a more positive way—talking about what you do want, instead of what you don't want—then, right away, the Highest Good will comply by starting to bring you the things that you're intending for."

"Wow!" she exclaimed. "Is that really all I have to do? Just by curtailing my complaints, I'll no longer

83

be drawing all those unwanted situations into my life. Instead, I'll be attracting the results into my future I'm really wanting for myself!" She was starting to get it. Her entire expression had shifted. Naomi was smiling now, whereas she'd been sullen and unresponsive earlier.

"Exactly!" I said. "It all has to do with what you put your attention on. When you place your attention on problems and unwanted experiences, that's what you'll be manifesting for yourself. However, when you hold your thoughts and words on the final outcomes you desire for yourself and others—on the best possible results you can imagine—then, that is what you'll begin to experience. It's the Law of Attraction, and it always works."

That conversation with Naomi took place a couple of months ago. Yesterday, as I was Christmas shopping in town, I ran into Naomi—and her new boyfriend. The look in her eyes said it all. She was happier than I'd ever seen her. It was a busy day, and we were both in a hurry, so we passed each other without saying a word. But, as she walked by, she winked at me as if to let me know that she'd taken our last conversation to heart. She was thinking and speaking more positively now, and her whole life reflected it.

You have to be able to converse
with people who are in a bind.

As we said, it really helps to hang out with friends who are also becoming more aware of what they're creating with their everyday thoughts and words. In this way, when one of us unconsciously says something that he really wouldn't want to be manifesting, a good friend might remind him by saying something like, *"Hey brother, you might not want to be saying that that way because it's just not going to give you the outcomes your looking for. How about if we rephrase your wording in a more positive light? For instance, instead of saying, 'I'm tired of being sick and unhappy all the time', you could say, 'I intend that I am living in perfect health, and I'm as happy as I can be!'"* In other words, we help each other, and in doing so, we create more desirable experiences for ourself and our fellow travelers. As a result, our lives are happier, more fulfilling, and more productive.

As successful as I've become in manifesting my intentions over the years, sometimes I still forget to make them. On last year's Intenders tour through the

Midwest, I stayed with my good friends, Gayle and Kenny, in Northwood, Iowa while I was preparing to lead an Intention Circle there. When I'm on the road, it's been my custom to seek out fresh fruit and veggies wherever I go. So on this beautiful sunny day, Gayle and I decided to take a drive in search of some fresh Iowa sweet corn.

Little did I realize that it was nearing the tail-end of the corn season, and as a result, the first three places we stopped were closed or sold out. I couldn't believe it: there was no doubt in my mind that we'd be coming home with a bag of delicious Iowa sweet corn. My mouth was already watering, and I was totally trusting in our intention to find the corn. But wait! I suddenly remembered that we hadn't actually made that intention. When I mentioned this to Gayle, we both went, "Duh!" and proceeded to state our intent that we find a fruit stand selling sweet corn, and that we are eating all the corn we want for supper that evening.

That's when Gayle suggested that the nearby town of Albert Lea might have some corn left; it was only 7 miles away, she said, and since we both love driving through the Iowa countryside, we agreed to check it out. No sooner had we pulled into the city limits of

*Albert Lea, right there on the first corner we came to
sat the only roadside stand within miles! Not only did
we load up on a dozen huge ears of delicious, Iowa
sweet corn, but we also brought home some of the best
cantaloupes I ever tasted.*

**Surround yourself with people
who are supportive
of where you are in your life now.**

{Remember}
Our Family Is Larger Than We Think

Sometimes we meet people and instantly feel
a sweet, but unexplained affinity with them. I was
recently in an Intenders Circle in Bentonville,
Arkansas (the home of Walmart) with a small
group of people, most of whom I'd never
previously met. The only longtime friend there
was a sprightly man named Bob who'd driven all
the way from Memphis, TN to be in the circle.
I'd known Bob from ten years earlier when he'd
invited us to his Unity Church in Memphis to show
them how we conducted an Intenders Circle. One
of his intentions that evening in Memphis many
years ago was that he would meet his soul mate

—the great love of his life. Now, here we were, together again, years later in Arkansas ... and Bob was accompanied by his beautiful wife, Joy, who was the answer to the intention he'd made back in Tennessee when I first met him!

Over the course of that evening in Walmart country, we all felt a closeness with each other that often happens in our Intenders Circles. The people felt wonderfully familiar, and I recall thinking that I'd like to be able to spend more time with them outside of our circle. Even Joy, who was new to this circle, noticed it, later saying, *"The meeting in Arkansas was 'otherworldly' for me. I felt as if I'd known each person there forever."*

Well, I was feeling the same way—and it flashed me back to one of our early Intenders Circles at Betsy's house in Pahoa, HI where we first started the Intenders. At that time, I was putting the finishing touches on my first book, an adventure novel about making and manifesting our intentions, and I didn't have a clear idea for the cover of the book. Since we'd be going to print soon, when it came my turn in the circle to say my intentions, I said, "I intend that I have a beautiful, attractive piece of art for the front cover of

88

my book; that it comes to me now, freely, easily, and effortlessly—and I love it!"

Typically, we were a small group of nine Intenders during our first year together, however on this particular evening, a stranger, Thierry Chatelain, showed up. Like many newcomers to our circles, Thierry was quiet at first, not saying much until I made my intention for the cover art for my book. Upon hearing my intention, he suddenly spoke up, telling us that he was an artist from San Diego, visiting friends in Hawaii, and had stumbled upon our little circle of Intenders almost by accident. His portfolio was out in the car. "Would you like to take a look at my work?" he asked me.

I said, "Yes!"—not really knowing what to expect.

As soon as Thierry brought his portfolio in and opened it, I knew the Highest Good (which I'd included in my intention-making) was at work. As it turned out, Thierry was famous, having his paintings on the Leaning Tree card racks in gift shops all over the country. The very first painting I turned to almost jumped off the page at me! It was called "Medicine Woman", and it had everything I wanted for the cover of my book. Even though we thumbed through the rest of Thierry's portfolio, "oooing and aaahing" at the quality of his work, I couldn't forget the Medicine Woman. Long story short, before the evening was over, Thierry and I struck up a deal permitting me to use this amazing piece of art on the front cover of my new book.

Much good comes to you
when you help each other.

Later that evening, when we were enjoying our weekly chat with Lee Ching, I mentioned the obvious synchronicity at work in our circle that night. It seemed like something magical was happening behind the scenes of our lives, bringing us together at just the right time for our intentions to manifest and our dreams to come true. I'll never forget Lee Ching's reply. He said, "Whenever you gather in these circles under the guidance and protection of the Highest Good, you call forth your soul group—those of you who have made agreements and arrangements, long ago, before you came into this lifetime, before you came into these bodies, for the purpose of supporting each other in this life."

No one said a word. We were all too excited about what he was saying to interrupt.

"Yes," he went on, "you have all come together, bonded by a common desire to rally around that which is called the Highest Good, in order to create something grand, something extraordinary in this lifetime. As I said, anytime a group of friends gathers together under the umbrella of the Highest Good, it calls forth your soul group. Therefore, if you're intending to know who else is in your soul group, you can always invoke the Highest Good, and they'll begin to show up in your life—just as Thierry has done here tonight. That's when you'll begin your true life's work."

"And what, exactly, is that work, Lee Ching?" I asked.

"You have all come to the Earth at this time to usher in a golden age of manifestation. Soul groups from all across the land are coming together and awakening to this wondrous project now at this most poignant time in your reckoning of history. They're gathering for the purpose of bringing light and love back into the forefront of the human experience during this unprecedented period of transition, a period when you will make the change from darkness to light, from separation to Oneness. This is what you came here to do ... and it all starts by coming into alignment with the Highest Good for one and all."

In the days ahead,
you will be helping each other
and working together
much more than you have in the past.
In this way, you'll be better prepared
for when it comes time
to make those stronger stands
for things like peace, equality, freedom,
sharing, and creating a pure,
pristine environment for yourselves.

{Remember}
People Are Different But Equal

Hierarchy works against the Highest Good. Our soul knows that we are all equal, and, at the same time, we are all different. It's our egos, in their desire to expand themselves, who claim that some of us are better than others. And while our individual egos see themselves as above everyone else, our soul cries out for balance. It's interesting to note that the great masses blindly accept hierarchy, even though it keeps us down, at a lower level of life. It does, however, provide us with the perfect training ground for realigning with our soul's calling and the Highest Good. Where else could we find such diversity and opportunity to overcome our unloving natures?

And that's exactly what we're dealing with: our unloving natures. From one point of view, life on this Earth offers us so many differences and distinctions to rise above. We see others as black and white, rich and poor, old and young, upper class and lower class. We see them as part of another religion, another nationality, another belief system—and all of this sets up an environment where we're given the opportunity to balance out our differences and realign with our soul's purpose for being here.

When people stop seeing themselves
up on a pedestal;
when they stop thinking,
"I'm up here and you're down there",
your world will be healed.

The Highest Good is love, not hate. We'll know when love is prevalent in our world when our racial prejudices, our insecurities, and our fear-motivated behaviors have given way to the caring and sharing that the Highest Good has to offer. That's the day when all life on Earth will breathe a huge sigh of relief; when we're released from the shackles of hierarchy. That's the day when all people, in all lands, will rejoice in the light of new worldly priorities dedicated to *Love, Life, Liberty and the true Pursuit of Happiness.*

That day is available right now as a vision we can hold in our minds that will ultimately work its way up to the surface of our worldly experience. All we have to do is keep asking ourselves the question: *Is what we're doing for our Highest Good?* When all the dust has settled, we'll know, in our hearts and minds, what the truthful answer to this question is. It's the one that makes us the happiest.

The Highest Good has only one requirement and that is to do what you came here to Earth to do, which is to love your fellow travelers. It's no more complicated than that. If, however, you're unloving in anyway, then you're out of alignment with your Highest Good, and you'll continue to have more work to do on yourself.

Love was with you when your body was born into this world, and it was with you when your soul was born from pure Spirit. All you need to do in order to come back to Love is to help the next person who is really in need. Help him take his next step in life. Help her find release from her woes. And at the same time, you must discern and refrain from judging the people and institutions who are harming, hurting, or hating others. For to judge those who hate is to prolong your own journey here on Earth – and to prolong theirs, as well.

In order to better understand this, you need to consider the Law of Cause and Effect. Instead of making so many judgments and constantly obsessing on what you perceive to be right and wrong, you can learn that whatever you cause will have its effects on you. Whatever you plant will surely be harvested. Whatever you do comes back to you later.

While this law is well known in the East, it is well hidden from us in the West. In its entirety, it says the reaping of that which you have sown is not confined to this present lifetime. Your harvests are meted out over the life of your soul. You come back, lifetime after lifetime, until you stop harming others or supporting others who are causing harm to others. You come back, again and again, until you learn to Love. This is what you're here for. This is how you come back in line with your personal Highest Good, as well as the Highest

Good for the whole of your world. This is what you
came here to do.

Lee Ching

The longer you hold to the old ways
where one profits at the expense of another,
the longer your challenges will continue.
However, as soon as you let go and allow
the Highest Good to bring about a solution
that is best for everyone,
your challenges will lessen.

{Remember}
Forgiving Is It's Own Reward

Much like mercy, forgiveness isn't honored in our world today. From the time we learn to speak, we're taught to seek revenge, to lash out at others who we think have harmed or offended us. Even though others may not have the slightest idea they've done anything to hurt us, that doesn't seem to matter nowadays to those who blindly seek an eye for an eye. Almost everyone in our culture supports a merciless, vengeful attitude, and there's only one problem with this: it won't bring us happiness.

Oh sure, some people may feel a bit of temporary relief upon exacting their revenge, but in the long run, their vengeful acts will invariably come back to bite them. The only way to achieve any lasting relief from these highly-charged circumstances is by learning to forgive. Forgiveness is the great comforter, cutting the cords to our earthly attachments and relieving us of the excess charge we've been carrying for all the unkind acts we think we've committed upon others, or that we think others have committed upon us. But what kind of forgiveness do we seek: the old way or the new way?

The old way of forgiving is when we perceive that someone else has wronged us, and we're needing to go to him and let him know that we no longer carry a grudge against him for what he did. Up until then, we'd been carrying around the hurt inside us, but we weren't quite ready to forgive him yet. Eventually, however, we realized that our excess emotional baggage from the hurtful incident was too much to bear, so we decided to give him a break, and let him off the hook by forgiving him for being so careless. We think that somehow everything will work out better if we lay it all on the line. This briefly summarizes the old way of forgiving.

The new forgiveness can be divided into two types: Self Forgiveness and Self-less Forgiveness. Self Forgiveness is used when we think someone else has hurt us, and Self-less Forgiveness is used when we think we may have harmed someone else. Let's first explore Self Forgiveness because it takes up where the old way of forgiving leaves off.

Self-Forgiveness
(to be applied when we think others have hurt us)

When we put Self Forgiveness to use, we go about ridding ourself of the emotional charge that we've been carrying around after we think someone has hurt us. As you'll see, Self Forgiveness takes two things into consideration: first, that we're all innocent and have never truly done anything wrong, except in our own minds; and second, that Self Forgiving happens inside us, and that the other person really has little or nothing to do with it. We're the ones carrying the excess emotional charge, so we're the ones in need of clearing ourselves of our emotional wounds. In other words, the hurt is within us, and that's where we need to do our forgiveness work.

Mainstream Miscreation #3 ~ Wrongdoing
How We Create Sin
(and how we can transmute it.)

Sometimes we have to go deeper in order to understand certain ideas that will set us free. Sin, or wrongdoing, cannot exist without first making a judgment—and making judgments is what's causing all the problems in our minds, in our lives, and in our world today. Conversely, when we're able to refrain from making a judgment, and we forgive others, we open a door that leads to freedom from all our earthly concerns.

It's not easy for some folks to understand the concept that they've never "sinned", and that "sin" doesn't really exist, except in their minds. I was having coffee the other day with my new friend, Thom, and he was telling me about his Catholic upbringing. He explained that, when he was young, he was an altar boy, and later on, he even spent a year in the seminary studying to become a priest before he met the woman of his dreams and decided to drop out and get married.

As the years went by, his studies branched out while he continued to search for the answers to life's spiritual questions. One day, he ran across a popular metaphysical book that said we're all innocent, and that we've never done anything wrong in the eyes of God. The book said that God doesn't judge us and that everyone goes to Heaven. Thom told me that this was such a foreign concept to him at first, especially after having had the belief in "sin" drummed into him from such an early age by the church, that he literally had to read the passages about innocence a hundred times in order to fully understand it. When it finally sunk in, he said it came with such a huge sigh of relief to know that he'd truly never done anything wrong, and that neither had anyone else. A feeling of peace, like he'd never before experienced, settled over him, and he was freed, from then on, from his self-imposed judgments of right and wrong.

Self-forgiveness frees us from our earthly attachments. For when we have learned to forgive, we'll be in harmony with the beautiful definition found in A Course in Miracles (ACIM), where

Jesus tells us, *"Forgiveness ... is still, and quietly does nothing ... It merely looks, and waits, and judges not."* In other words, when judgmental thoughts of wrongdoing pop up in our mind, we forgive them by *overlooking* them and going back to whatever we were doing. In this way, we're not feeding our judgments. We're not giving them any energy, so, in time, they'll go away on their own.

> *You can clean and cleanse your life*
> *so that you are walking around in sublime bliss.*

I was chatting recently with a very pleasant young man named Marshall. He was distraught and ready to give up on life because of the way he was being treated at his church. As his story unfolded, I discovered that he was the church's music director, but the pressures to conform on all levels of life weighed heavily upon him. The church elders didn't like the music he arranged; the board members rubbed him the wrong way; even his marriage suffered because his wife wasn't happy when he brought all of his problems from the church home every evening. In short, he was beaten down by all the things he thought he was doing wrong.

As you can imagine, Marshall is a sensitive, soft-spoken man, easily affected by the pressures of his peers. I listened to his woes for a long time, then suggested that he see himself as innocent. "You've never done one thing wrong in your life," I told him. "Your guilt is something you carry around in your own heart and mind, and those are the places you need to work on in order to free yourself from it. Throughout your life, others have done their best to make you feel wrong, or sinful, or guilty, so they could control you and get you to do what they wanted you to do. The truth, however, is that you're as innocent as a newborn babe. You've never done anything wrong; **you just think that you have.**"

His response was immediate and powerful. It blew me away. "You're crazy!" he said. "I've done a lot of things wrong in my life! I've hurt people. I haven't done what they wanted. I've sinned over and over again. That's why the elders want me out of the church!"

His vehemence took me aback, but my knowing of my own innocence (as well as his) was so strong that I realized he was arguing on behalf of his limitations. He was holding on to his guilt to the point where it was affecting every aspect of his life: his work, his marriage, his inner happiness. "I've got an idea," I said to him.

"What if you forgave all of the situations where you see yourself being wrong? What if, whenever the thoughts or pressures from others come into your mind, you simply overlooked them."

"I can't do that!" he said. "It just isn't part of my make-up. It's not how I was raised. How can I be innocent after all the sins I've committed? I can't just overlook them."

Out of respect for Marshall, we won't go into the nature of his "sins" here, however, it's important to note that he is not a murderer, or an abuser, or a criminal in any way. On a scale from one to ten, his supposed wrongdoings, to me, would have been a zero, and yet they were draining his life so much that I couldn't help but feel great compassion for him. "You can change your mind, Marshall," I finally said. "One thought is just as accessible to you as another. You can choose to take the church elders less seriously when they pressure you. You can remember that you are free, in your own mind, to see yourself as innocent or guilty—and I'd suggest that you'll be a lot happier if you choose on the side of your innocence"

"I just can't do that," he repeated as firmly as before. "It's just not me!"

At that point, I realized that I needed to take another

tack. It was highly unlikely that he was going to let go of his thoughts of having "sinned" right away. It would take time. "You know, Marshall," I said, "I really want to help you, and I can see that I'm just making you more upset by sharing these ideas with you. Perhaps it would be best if we changed the subject, or called it a day. In the meantime, I'm going to do something that may help you. Rather than taking anymore of your time right now, I'm going to go home tonight and have a talk with my angels, and I'm going to ask them to get together with your angels to resolve your situation. I do this in the name of God and the Highest Good for everyone concerned. Is that alright with you?"

In that instant, Marshall's whole demeanor shifted. His adversarial attitude went away. A feeling of peace settled in, as tears welled up in his eyes. I didn't say a word while he wept for several minutes. When he was done, I silently thanked God for the lessons we were both learning. Everything got better for both of us when I remembered to step aside and call on the Highest Good.

**Sometimes it's best to give others
a chance to discover things on their own.**

We rid ourselves of our guilt by Self Forgiving. Whenever a thought of wrongdoing or having sinned comes into our mind, we can either *clear* it out by tracing it back to its source, or we can *overlook* it entirely—and in this way we're not giving it any more power over us; we're no longer fueling the fires of our own guilt. We're no longer complicit in creating our own unhappiness. The good thing is that, like meditation, it's a cumulative process. The more we learn to shift our attention, *overlook* our judgmental, unforgiving thoughts, and reclaim our innocence, the sooner our guilt will melt away and be replaced by a feeling of happiness, a feeling we never could have experienced as long as we weren't forgiving ourself.

Self-less Forgiveness
(to be applied when we think we have hurt others)

We put Self-less Forgiveness to use when we think we've done something that's caused someone else to be holding emotional charge because we've hurt them. Our intent with Self-less Forgiveness is to clear the air, so to speak, so we're no longer connected to them because of the hurtful incident. In spiritual jargon, it's our intention to clear up the effects of the past hurtful experiences that have tied us together energetically by cutting the karmic cords between us, so we can both fly free.

Self-less Forgiveness often requires us to be resourceful and tailor our approach to others somewhat delicately. We begin by contacting the people who may be holding a grudge against us, and then we do our best to make amends. We can see them in person, but, if that's not possible, we can call or email them and tell that we apologize for having harmed them in any way. We can tell them that we acted unlovingly back then, and we'd like to clear the air. We admit to our careless behavior and offer to do whatever we can to help them. We do this by asking them if there is anything they want or need.

Love is putting our attention on others
the way they want it put on them,
not necessarily the way
we want to put it on them.

At this point, they may tell us one of several things. They might say that all is forgiven and released—and that will be the end of it. Or, they might ask a favor of us, or tell us that they need help in some way. Here, we have to be open to make our amends in anyway we can. Having our lingering emotional wounds resolved depends on it. So, if they need a material object, we should do our best to get it for them. If they live nearby and need personal help, we should do our best to do what they ask. We should not hold back at this point because here is where the "karmic cords" are cut.

Even if we're unable to grant their specific wish, we can send them a gift with a card of apology, making sure that the gift is something we think they would appreciate. At the very least, we should get their address and send a note of thanks for their understanding. These things are more than symbolic; they actually break the ice and open the way for the other person to forgive us.

And one more thing: it's important that we make absolutely no effort, beyond the act of forgiveness itself, to rekindle our relationship with them at this time. It cannot be our purpose to do anything but to make amends. Any effort on our part to get them to relate with us beyond this act of Self-less Forgiveness will tend to sabotage everything we've just done. We need only to make amends and go on our way. This is what completes the cycle of cause and effect.

Not too long ago, I was in a relationship with a lovely lady named Margie. We were hot and heavy for the first year, and the only thing that ever bothered me was once, when she told me that if I ever left her, she would never forgive me. Well, I forgot about this, but after another year our bond began to sour, and one day I up and left. I don't even remember the exact cause for my leaving; I just knew, even though she'd done nothing specific to antagonize me, that it was time for me to get away.

I've been single since then and have been working on myself to resolve my old issues and get clear of them. So when I realized that there were still some unhappy feelings between me and Margie, I built up my courage and called her one evening, apologized, and asked her to forgive me for leaving her so suddenly. She didn't say anything at first, so I asked her if there was anything I could do to clear things up between us. I said, in all honesty, that I wasn't calling to try to get back together with her, but that I just wanted to be friends. Could I help her with anything in her life right then?

I think my offer caught her by surprise because she seemed to warm up to me, and as it turned out, she mentioned that the camera she used in her photography business had just broken, and she really needed another one. Right away, I got her new address and said I'd take care of it. What kind did she need?

We chatted for a few more minutes, and when we hung up, I felt a lot better. The next day I went out and bought her the camera she needed, and I mailed it to her with a note apologizing again, and telling her that it was great talking with her. A week and a half later, she called me back and thanked me profusely. The gratitude in her voice opened me up, and even though she'd told me back when we were together that she would never forgive me, the emotions running through my body after her call told me otherwise. I felt completely released—and I think she did, too.

Joe Paresi

Always ask for and intend to have your freedom.

In order to better understand the Self-less Forgiveness process, let's play a short imaginary game. Think of a person you have likely harmed in your life, and picture yourself approaching him (or her) and apologizing for your thoughtless behavior in the past. You needn't say you're sorry because it isn't necessary or helpful for you to feel sorrow in situations like this. Just see him forgiving you, and let that settle in for a moment. Then see how you feel. You should be feeling a noticeable relaxation in your midsection. Your emotional center should feel more open now, like it's relieved of an old wound that's being healed. Now you have a small taste of what it will be like when you actually approach this person in real life. The great by-product of forgiveness always comes in the form of a lighter, brighter feeling in our body. Now we're detached from our old emotional baggage, baggage we may have been carrying around with us for eons.

Life is a process.
It's not a timeline that begins at our birth
and ends at our death.

Freedom Is Inside Us

We have to learn to stand in the middle of the tempests and remain calm and centered, regardless of whatever is going on around us. This juggling act is one of the most important issues facing humanity today; indeed, the people who can stay calm during the storms of life are the ones who are getting free from the treadmill that others are stuck on. They aren't swayed by what others think of them. They march to their own tune.

As we've said, we are free, inside our minds, to think whatever we want to think. Even though someone bigger or more powerful than us may be telling us what we should be thinking, the final decision is up to us. *We can think what we want, and, therefore, we can create conditions inside ourselves that lead to our happiness and fulfillment.* We needn't feel obligated to go along with the crowd, unless we feel like our immediate physical well-being is being threatened (although it's sometimes wise to remain silent when we're standing toe-to-toe with a nasty scoundrel.) And even then, when we're faced with the tyrants and scoundrels of the world, we can learn to be at peace within ourself. As a matter of fact, it's when we're in the midst of our greatest challenges that our highest ideals come to the surface. Sometimes in the "pitch and roll" of the world's craziest conditions, we discover our greatest opportunities to rise up and out of it all.

Oftentimes things may be happening all around you
that seem to be discordant,
and you cannot imagine what's going on.
But you must remain focused and steadfast,
and be able to see through,
and not get caught up in all the mundane dramas
that are constantly being perpetuated on this planet.

Many people nowadays are learning to locate their calm in the center of the storms of life and stay there until the craziness lets up. Indeed, there comes a time in all of our lives when we ask ourselves whether we'd prefer the storms, or whether we would prefer the peace that's inside us. This is when it's wise to check in with our inner guidance and ask ourself whether it's for our Highest Good, and the Highest Good of all concerned, to get involved in the activities and obligations of the world—or whether it's in our Highest Good to withdraw into the silence of our own mind where we are free, and ride out the rest of the storm from there.

Mainstream Miscreation #4
Financial Obligations
How We Create Debt
(and how we can transmute it.)

Let's be clear. Debt is slavery. It's the means by which we allow someone else to gain control over us for an extended length of time. It encumbers us for years, often for the whole of our lives, relentlessly taking our energy away every thirty days in the form of contracted, recurring monthly payments.

Money represents our material energy. We accumulate it by various means and spend it on the things we need to survive and thrive. Our homes, our vehicles, our education, and many of our larger expenditures are purposely designed to be too costly for us to save up for, so we have to borrow money in order to live a more comfortable lifestyle. The challenge with this system is that every thirty days rolls around very quickly, and we have to find a way to pay back the money we've borrowed before the next thirty-day cycle takes over—and woe be unto us if we're late or unable to pay on time. Fines are levied, credit scores adjusted, interest rates raised, creditors begin calling—all in the name of business— while the debtor (you and me) has to scramble, and perhaps work harder, or take on another job, in order to satisfy the merciless creditors. The sad part is that most folks live out their entire lives under the yolk of ever-mounting debt, diligently paying each month, only to have the credit companies penalize them even more when they get sick or old.

Last year, my wife passed away and I didn't realize that she'd stopped paying the monthly bills when she was too sick to do so. As it turned out, she missed one payment to Big Buy for a computer and a camera we'd purchased on credit years before. I called the offices of Big Buy Credit Services as soon as I found out what happened, but they were totally unforgiving. They said that I'd just missed the due date by three days and, as a result, they decided to drastically increase my interest rate. By the time I was off the phone, I discovered that 50% of every one of my monthly payments would now be going toward the interest on the debt, a debt that still burdens me to this day after paying on it for almost ten years. At my age, unless I come into an unexpected inheritance, I don't see how this bill will ever be completely paid off in my lifetime.

Charlie McGregor

Our Founding Fathers warned us against the horrors of usury—the interest we're charged on the money we borrow. They foresaw exactly what is happening in our business world today, and they knew that uncaring creditors would use any excuse to squeeze more money from their borrowers, no different than they did a hundred years ago when they lashed and thrashed anyone who couldn't pay. Isn't it time we put an end to this system of recurring debt once and for all? But how?

The answer is: by intending it, envisioning it, and holding that vision until it manifests in real life. For the day will come, in the not-too-distant future, when we've replaced loaning with giving, and when borrowing has no strings attached. In the meantime, however, we must realize that our true freedom is not dependant on what's going on in our external world; it's to be found inside us by forgiving the tyrants and creditors of the world. For when we can stop judging these people and be grateful for the services they're providing, we set ourselves firmly on a path to freedom, a freedom that can only be found within us.

Even the prisoner in a jail cell
can be free in his heart and mind,
if he intends it for himself.

In the East, it's common for people to define their freedom in terms of knowing who they are. They say once a person is able to go inside and discover their true Spiritual Essence that all their previous definitions for freedom fade away. When they've realized that they are not their body—that they are the Essential Being currently located inside the body—then they can begin to be free from the body's wants and needs.

So, how do we break free from the body and our identification with it? You've heard the wise saying, *"Be still and know that I am God."* When we apply it to ourself, it not only refers to holding our mind still, but it also refers to holding our body still. For once we can sit, or lay down and be completely still for a period of time—in both our body and our mind—the Essence of who we really are will reveal itself. For some, this may take years of practice, while for others it may only take a few minutes. In either case, it's the promise of those who have gone before us that when we are totally still in body and mind, our Highest Good comes forth and shows us who we are. It shows us that we are free, that we are Love, and that we are One with all things.

There is so much suffering in your world, but it doesn't have to be that way. You could be happy and free and enjoy completely fulfilled lives. There are worlds in your universe where freedom does exist and is honored by all. There are many such worlds.

On the surface, your earthly suffering is caused because you're unforgiving. Fortunately for those who can refrain from judging and be still, peace can come. There is hope. You can seek a place within where you are untouched by your world. It is a place unbounded by limits and unreachable to those who cling to their selfish ways. As close as your own body, yet as distant as the farthest star, it calls to you. It says look in your heart. Look deep into your heart. There you will find your peace, your freedom, your release from all suffering.

As you walk this world, let not its troubles and tribulations walk with you. Walk in the knowing that the day will come when your freedom and all you have longed for will be yours. It is with you even now as you tread upon this Earth. It is with you always.

Lee Ching

**Spend more time looking within
rather than looking without.**

{Remember}
Gifts Are Ours For The Asking

Over the years, many of our intentions have become household words, but perhaps none more than *"I intend that I am guided, guarded, protected, and lined up with the Highest Good at all times"*. People love this phrase; we know this because we often hear it in our Intenders Circles, phone conversations, and emails. Something about it resonated deeply in all of us from the first time Lee Ching brought it to our attention.

A few weeks back I received a download from Lee Ching telling me we could make a change to our "guided, guarded, and protected" intention. He said that because so many people are being challenged to make ends meet nowadays, they needed "a boost" to their intention making. That "boost", he said, involved us adding the words "provided for" into the Fourth Intent of The Code*, so that now it will say "I intend that I am guided, guarded, protected, provided for, and lined up with the Highest Good at all times."

After that, I took Lee Ching's advice and started including the words "provided for" into my daily intentions, and I can't tell you how much it has helped me! All sorts of things have come into my life since then—new friends, unexpected donations, more food on the pantry shelves, etc. I feel more abundant. It's like I'm breathing a huge sigh of relief now that I've been intending that I'm provided for.

If you're ever feeling like you're unloved, not cared for, or not provided for, we recommend that

you take this intention and use it for yourself.
It really makes a difference. As Lee Ching says,
"You'll see!"

The Fourth Intent of The Code: Simplify
I let go so there is room
for something better to come in.
I intend that I am guided,
guarded, protected, provided for,
and lined up with the Highest Good at all times.
I trust and remain open to receive from both
expected and unexpected sources. I simplify.

*You can download a free 8.5x11 color poster of
The Code: 10 Intentions for a Better World at:
http://www.highestlighthouse.com/TheCode.html.

{Remember}
Prayers And Intentions Work

People ask what my life has been like since I intended
to live by manifesting — and the answer is: I've had the
most amazing ride imaginable! I've lived on the beach
in Hawaii; amid towering red rocks outside Payson,
AZ; atop Big Avocado Mountain in Escondido, CA;

in the Shasta Valley with majestic Mt. Shasta framed in my picture window. I've camped across America several times, vacationed from the Caribbean to Bora Bora, bathed in luxury in Corrales, NM, basked in the powerful vortices of Sedona, AZ, (before it got crowded), and restored my Spirit on the banks of the Willamette River near Eugene, OR. I've taken part in Intention Circles across the country in private homes, churches of all denominations, community centers, social clubs, gift shops, Grange halls, Masonic lodges, casinos, hotels, public parks, and book stores galore. In short, I've made more friends than I ever thought possible, traveled to places I only dreamed of, and lived in some of the most magnificent spots on Earth, all of which manifested following intentions I made for the Highest Good.

TB

In order for your intentions to manifest, you have to believe they will. If you don't, the material in this book is unlikely to help you. If, however, you have within you even the smallest belief when you make an intention that it will manifest for you, then prepare to take your next step in life. Make an intention, and you'll see. If it's for your Highest Good, it'll manifest. Then, when it comes to life, be ready to acknowledge the direct relationship between the making of your intention and the manifestation of it. When you can do this, everything in your life clicks into place. Most folks tend to let the acknowledgment of the manifestation of their intentions slip by. We forget to notice that the thing we just manifested was caused by an intention we made earlier. This little oversight can be very costly for us until we remember to express our acknowledgments. How would we ever get more proficient in our intending unless we're paying attention to our successes? We need to acknowledge our WINS if we're going to build confidence and proficiency.

There was a time when I diligently wrote down all of my intentions on a piece of paper that was taped to a shelf that slid out from the front of my desk. A few years went by and I'd almost forgotten about it, but last month, when I was downsizing and getting ready to sell the desk, I pulled out the shelf with my old list of intentions on it, and it surprised me how many of them had manifested over the years. Not all of them, mind you, but most of them had manifested for me,

and as I looked back, I was just as grateful for the ones
that hadn't manifested. They clearly would not have
been for my Highest Good.

Don Haskins

The best way to acknowledge our manifestations is by expressing our gratitude. When we're grateful for an intention that just manifested, it opens the door for more manifestations to follow. *Our gratitude becomes the engine that keeps the cycle going. We make an intention; we see it manifest; we acknowledge it by being grateful for it. And we do it all again. The trick is to keep doing it; keep making intentions until you're so confident in it that it becomes part of your life.* After that, all you have to do is be open to receive, and let the Highest Good take over—and that's when things get really good! You'll begin to make intentions everyday, and throughout the day, as needed. Your problems are resolved because you've intended their solutions. Your needs are met because you've intended that they're taken care of. Now that you're more aware of the link between your intention-making and your manifestations, you feel more empowered, better able to deal with the challenges of life. Life

gets fun again. Why wouldn't it? You're getting
what you want.

As soon as you see things in a new way,
with a perspective of gratitude
and an opportunity for growth,
you will be rewarded immensely.

*Our next door neighbors were getting on in years
and weren't able to mow their small lawn anymore.
They had a really nice, newer lawnmower, and so they
made a deal with my teenage son: If he would take care
of their yard and mow their lawn in the summer, they
would trade him their mower.*

*As it turned out, my son, who was struggling at the
time, but reading my Intenders Handbook to find some
direction in his life, was much more resourceful than
we expected. After mowing our next door neighbors'
lawn, he made an intention to start a neighborhood
lawn-mowing business, cutting the grass for the other
people who lived down our block. He ended up with a
thriving neighborhood yard service and made enough
spending money for the summer so that I didn't have
to give him an allowance—and, at the same time, he
wasn't struggling or bored anymore. We're so grateful*

—and it all happened because of an intention he made, and the kindness of our next door neighbors.

Brent Lundgren

The Intention Process is the *Law of Attraction* put to practical use. It says that we'll become more proficient at manifesting our dreams and desires when we do three things: 1) Say our intentions or prayers every morning; 2) Get together with friends every week or so, and say our intentions or prayers into a circle; and 3) Line all our intentions or prayers up with the Highest Good by including the Highest Good phrase in with our intention making.

The Intenders Beginner's Luck Factor has just outdone itself again! I was chatting with our new Oklahoma Intenderpreneur, Cliff, about how his fledgling Intenders Circle was going. You see, most of our Intenders Circles last several years, with people, especially in the beginning, manifesting all sorts of things. We call it our Beginner's Luck Factor because Lee Ching told us that, whenever we gather under the auspices of the Highest Good, it calls forth invisible forces who rally to our side and see to it that our first few intentions are manifested, so there's absolutely no mistaking it.

Cliff's Circle was only a little over a month old, so it surprised me when he told me that they'd stopped meeting for the time being. When I asked him why, he said, "because we already manifested everything we intended for!"

Later, when I asked Lee Ching about this, he explained that there's a lot more going on in our Intenders Circles than meets the eye. He told us that not only would we be manifesting our dreams and desires, but that we were also gathering for the purpose of enjoying the great benefits community has to offer. He emphasized that when the time comes for us to put our manifesting skills to the test on a higher level, we would be ready because of our experiences in our Intenders Circles.

So, what do people do after they've manifested everything they've intended for? It's a question we frequently get in our Intenders workshops, and it's worth exploring. Since these Intenders materials are specifically designed to help you get more proficient at manifesting, it follows that many of you would have taken advantage

126

of this information over the years and, having manifested all your desires, would be asking yourselves, *"What's next?"*

The answer is to be found in *an extraordinary experience,* in a new way of looking at ourself. The Highest Good asks us to seek out our highest potential, a potential that transcends any mainstream values in favor of a new vision that leads to an expansion of who we think we are. It calls upon us to go beyond our old boundaries and open ourselves up to possibilities heretofore undreamed of.

BJ said that once we've gotten everything we ever wanted, there's a great temptation to control people.

"After a person has had all the money, the lovers, the fancy cars, the travels, the yachts, the houses in the south of France, the possessions, pills, and powders ... what does he or she do next?" He asked me this one morning as we were getting ready to build a deck onto the front of my rustic Kona coffee shack.

Before I could respond, he answered his own question. "Some are tempted to manipulate the masses; they want to move blocks of people around, like pieces on a chessboard. These are typically the ones without compassion or conscience," he said, then paused for a moment. "Others," he went on, "have transcended the tendency to manipulate people. Instead, they intend to love people and, ultimately, they turn inside, in search of the miraculous."

After all is said and manifested, the Highest Good guides us toward our true destiny. We're being led to answer a higher purpose, one that takes us to the next step in our evolution. That's the promise the Highest Good makes to those who intend for *win-win* outcomes, where all parties in every situation are happy and satisfied. That's the gift the Highest Good makes to those who are willing to care about others as much or more than themselves. It's no longer about the Highest Good for the few. The Highest Good for all men, women, and children who live and breathe on this magnificent Earth is the bedrock upon which we stand.

Here's the key: once you know, without any equivocation, that you stand for *Love, Life, Liberty and the Pursuit of Happiness*—not just for yourself,, but for everyone else, too—then the Highest Good immediately goes to work on your behalf. After that, all you have to do is hang on for the ride and see what's around the next bend. You may be pleasantly surprised.

Truly, you are moving toward something much greater than your desires.

{Remember}
See And Feel
Your Intentions Manifesting

Once we make an intention we have to be ready for it to manifest. We must expect it. This doesn't mean that we'll know all the specific details: the color, size, or shape of what we're intending for. In fact, we can leave those things up to the Highest Good, and let ourselves be pleasantly surprised at how well the Highest Good knows what's best for us. Of course, there's nothing wrong with being specific when we envision our intentions coming into physical creation. However, what's just as important as envisioning every little detail is feeling the feeling that accompanies the manifestation of our intentions.

After twenty-five years of working in the field

of conscious manifesting via intention-making, we in the Intenders can tell you that the better you are at conjuring up the feelings, in advance, of the joy, the love, or the fulfillment that will be running through your body at the time of your manifestation, the easier manifesting will be for you. Said another way, if, at the time you're originally making your intention (or saying your prayer), you can bring up the way you're going to feel at the moment your dream actually comes true, and hold that feeling for as long as you can, then you're on your way to becoming a master manifestor.

Picture and feel
the end result from the very beginning.

The great masters know to hold the emotion of what it will be like when their intention has already manifested. They know, too, to hold an image in their mind of what it will be like when their intention has manifested. They make good use of both their mind *and* their feelings in order to become proficient at the art of conscious creation. What we Intenders have found is that, when we make an intention, if we can hold the vision *and* the feeling of it having already manifested for at least two or three minutes, then we greatly accelerate the manifestation process. The longer we're able to hold that vision and feeling, the quicker and easier our intentions and prayers will be answered.

I meditate every morning before starting my day, and then I say my intentions right after coming out of my quiet time, while I'm still in that dreamy, half-awake / half-meditative state of awareness. That way, the distractions of the day haven't kicked in yet, so it's easier for me to focus on holding my thoughts and feelings on the object of my intentions.

Last weekend, when I came out of my meditation and said my intentions for the day, I took a few extra minutes to both see and feel a nice check arriving in the mail. I actually felt the excitement and joy as I envisioned myself opening the envelope and seeing the $500 I'd intended for written on the check. Then, after I was satisfied that I'd taken long enough to set my intention in motion, I turned it over to the Highest Good and let it go.

Yesterday afternoon — four days later — I was

visiting with an old friend who asked me how my work was going. When I said fine, but that things at work had been slower lately, she got up, walked over to a nearby table, picked up an envelope, and handed it to me. Inside was a check for $500—the exact amount I'd intended for! I can't tell you how good it felt—not only because of the money, but also for the confirmation that the Intention Process was working so beautifully in my life. The only difference came in the way the check was delivered. It didn't arrive in the manner I'd envisioned. I thought it was going to come in the mail, but the Highest Good must have known I'd appreciate it even more if it was delivered by hand from a friend.

Randy Fredrich

Taking it a step further, now that we've become more proficient at matching the feelings we expect to be enjoying at the moment our intention is manifesting, we're finding that these feelings become considerably more accessible to us than they were before. With practice, we've learned to raise our vibration by deliberately calling forth the feelings of joy and happiness. We don't need to have an object or physical manifestation in mind; we can go directly to the place inside us where we feel good and stay there. Since we're lined up with the Highest Good, it's much easier for us to tap into our "high heart"—the place in the center of our chest where our sweetest feelings reside. With a bit more practice, we soon discover a direct connection between the sweetest of our feelings and the Highest Good. The Highest Good has been pointing us to our high heart all along.

Look deep inside yourself. Follow the thread of who you are to its origin. Open your heart wider and from its center core, expand it outward now so that the feeling residing there spreads in all directions. Expand it to your front and behind you, to your right and to your left. Now there is no area of your upper body untouched by the radiant love coming forth from the center of your heart.

Breathe into this feeling and expand it further. Let it encompass your whole body. Let it encompass your whole awareness. Now the sweetness of love surrounds you as you surround it. Bask in its light. Bathe in its joy. Be humbled in its presence. No other feeling on Earth compares to the glorious expansion of love that issues forth from the human heart.

So profound is this expansion that spiritual teachers

the world over revere it as Divine. That is why it is deemed sacred in all religions. That is why Jesus points to his loving heart. And that is why it is called the home of the most holy. For in the very center of your heart lies the seed of all that you long for ... and as your seed opens and begins to grow, it is God in all Her radiance Who is revealed to you. You need look no further than the center of your own expanded heart to find all that you seek.

Lee Ching

{Remember}
Miracles Are Our Birthright

One of the first things Lee Ching told us was, *"The time is coming when you will have a thought and it will be there."* At that point in my life, this statement didn't make much sense to me. I knew there was a relationship between my thinking and my experiencing, but the idea that, someday, the manifestation of my experiences would be coming right on the heels of my thoughts was quite another thing. Back when we were first starting the Intenders, it seemed like it took a long time for a thought or an intention to manifest. It was as if I'd be drumming my fingers and waiting for weeks or months for some of the things I'd intended for to come into my physical reality. Not any more! Now, a quarter of a century later, Lee Ching's words are ringing true. With each passing day, the speed at which our thoughts are manifesting is increasing faster and faster. So much so that we can make an intention, turn around, and practically bump into whatever it was we've been intending to manifest.

I'm writing this book not knowing "how" the money will come for printing it when it's finished. I just know it'll come. The "how" is not my business. In fact, worrying about the "how" only seems to get in the way of my intending and manifesting.

Experience has taught me that as long as I'm diligent and following my calling in life (for me, it's writing books and giving uplifting talks), then the funds will follow so the creative project I'm working on can be completed without a hitch. Naturally, there's a tendency to fall back into my old ways of thinking I need "to do something" in order to earn the money to reprint my books. However, I've learned, by going through the creative process many times, that everything I need will be there for me precisely when it's needed. Why? Because I've intended it.

I generally print about 3000 to 4000 copies of The Intenders Handbook at a time because the cost per book is much less when I print in these quantities. The first time I ran out of handbooks—which are my bread and butter—I was in Tucson and made an intention in our circle that night that I have the $5000 required to reprint my handbook. Within seconds, a man named Ron spoke up from across the circle, saying, "Tony, I'll gladly give you $5000 to reprint your book." I could have jumped out of my shorts! The feeling that ran through my body was entirely beyond words. Thank you, Ron!

The second time I ran out of handbooks, I was in my hometown of Pagosa Springs, Colorado in a circle of friends, and I made the exact same intention I'd made in Tucson a few years earlier. On this occasion, a beautiful, elderly lady named Pat came to my rescue. She invited us to come to her office the next day, and when we arrived, she handed me an envelope with $5000 in it. It had happened again—and my level of trust was growing exponentially! Thank you, Pat!

The third time I needed to reprint, I was getting

*ready to go on tour and was down to less that a hundred copies to take on the road with me. A few days before leaving, I received a call from a lady from Prescott, AZ named Judy who wanted to know if I would come to Orlando to present the keynote speech to the National Conference of the American Massage Therapists Association. The speech (you can watch it on Youtube entitled **Manifestation and the Law of Agreement**) came with an advance payment of $5000—more than enough to reprint my handbooks and enjoy an extra playday at Disneyworld after the conference. Thank you, Judy!*

In short, every time my inventory was running low, and I've needed to print or reprint any of my three (now four) handbooks, the money has always come from sources I never would have expected. And every time the money came, my level of trust increased to the point where, nowadays, *my trust has turned into a knowing*. I just *know*, if it's for the Highest Good, that my intentions will manifest at the perfect, right time. It may have taken a quarter of a century for me to get to this point, but it's been well worth the journey.

When you're in the moment,
and you follow your heart,
and you follow your soul,
you're always taken care of.

Instant manifestations are occurring more and more in our lives, and it's causing us to be considerably more vigilant about what we're thinking. I remember when Lee Ching first told us that the speeding up of our thought manifestations would be happening someday. In truth, many of us were confused by the idea of it. Fortunately, it was around that same time that he was introducing us to the concept of the Highest Good. *"The Highest Good,"* he said, *"is your saving grace. If you can allow yourself to be guided, and you rely upon your knowing that the outcome will be for your Highest and Best Good, your confusion will fade, and you will become clear. The Highest Good will always send you in the right direction."*

Twenty-five years later, we have found that to be true.

You are learning to trust from a very deep level
that which you may not have trusted before.

Trust Gives Us Power

Most folks are knee-deep in their worries about "how" the things they want or need are going to come to them. Unfortunately, worrying works against us. When we worry it means that we're fearful that our intention won't manifest. We're seeing it being restricted or blocked in some way. As a result, in imagining all the things that could interfere, we disavow our trust in the Intention Process, and we short-circuit the manifestation of our dreams.

You are learning that once you intend something,
and it is in your highest and best good,
it will make itself available to you.
If, however, you are still believing in fear or suffering
more than you believe in the Highest Good,
you will be experiencing more of that.

Trust is what we Intenders use in place of worry. We trust that the things we've intended for will come as needed. We also trust that things can come to us from unexpected sources, just as easily as from the expected ones. This is the difference between the Master Intender and the novice. The Master is open for things to come from anywhere, while the newbie limits himself by thinking that things can only come from predetermined sources.

Last year, right before I had to leave to go traveling, I was running here and there, having fun with friends, and overdoing it on all levels. In short, I needed to do some detoxing and clean my body out of all the things I'd been putting into it lately so I'd be at my best in front of my upcoming audiences. At the same time, my angelic white kitty, Opal, died following a prolonged illness, and when I was burying her in the backyard, I was bitten on the foot by a centipede. It put me in bed for five days dealing with intense pain and having to crawl to the bathroom on my hands and knees ... and I was scheduled to make a keynote speech in Michigan in two weeks! The only thing to do was lay there and start to clean out the insect poison, as well as all the other toxins I'd been putting into my body recently—and **trust** that everything would turn out okay.

When the pain subsided enough for me to be able to think clearly, the first thing I did was make an

*intention for the Highest Good that I am perfectly
healthy for my trip east. Long story short, a week and
a half later, I got well just in time to pack the car (I
don't do airplanes), and drive away, the drive giving
me plenty of time to continue detoxing, as well as to
think about why all of this happened to me.*

*Checking in with Lee Ching as I drove, he told
me that my team of invisible helpers saw to it that I
purified before my travels by having a bug bite me
in order to get me to slow me down and detox. He
went on to elaborate, saying that the Highest Good
always has ways of keeping us on our path in life.
When we stray from that path, the Highest Good will
take measures to redirect us. He said that we make
agreements and arrangements before we come into
this life to accomplish certain soul goals, and when
we're lined up with the Highest Good, we'll be helped
in ways we can't imagine. In fact, the Highest Good
will do whatever is necessary to safely realign us with
our chosen destiny.*

*In my case, it took a nasty centipede bite to slow
me down and clean me out—but it worked. I recovered
and healed, had a great tour, made new friends, and
introduced a lot of people to the win-win benefits of the
Highest Good along the way. My life's calling is back*

on track, and I can't tell you how grateful I am to the invisible members of my soul family for taking such good care of me, bug bite and all.

Looking back on the entire experience, I wouldn't be surprised if Opal arranged the whole thing...

> **These times of great change**
> **call upon all of those who are holding the light**
> **to set an example for others**
> **by being happy and uplifted,**
> **regardless of the circumstances around them.**

Life is not meant to be hard. We make it so by our thoughts and our immoderate activity. We believe and behave in ways that don't serve us. Fortunately, behind the scenes of our lives, the Highest Good transcends our *miscreations*, guiding us every step of the way, although we typically don't recognize it. It's constantly shining down on the oppressed and starving peoples of the Earth, just as it shines on the pomp and powerful. It shines on the wealthy, as well as the wanderer, presenting the way out of all oppressive situations. Naturally, if we're way out of balance, there may be times while adjustments are being made, and we may even undergo some hardship or another. But it's without a doubt that, as long as we trust in the Highest Good, it will deliver us back to where we started, back onto the path we set for ourself before we came here.

Mainstream Miscreation #5 ~ Hard Times
How We Create Scarcity
(and how we can transmute it.)

How many times have you heard someone say, "Times are hard"? And how many times did you buy into it? It's in our Highest Good to be aware of how we react in these situations because whenever we believe in hard times, we're creating them for ourselves. At our core, we're unlimited beings capable of thinking anything and, therefore, creating anything. Why, then, would we ever want to agree with anyone else that times are hard? Times are only hard for us when we believe they are. If we choose to believe and behave as if times are hard, then that is what we'll experience. However, when we stand strong in our belief that times are good, then that is what we'll be creating for ourselves. Either way, it's what we believe, in the sanctity of our own mind, that gives rise to our daily experiences.

Fortunately, whatever is going on out in the world need not affect how we think, unless we allow it to do so. It matters not if someone else wants to hold onto their "hard times" attitude. As the light-workers of our time, it's up to us to hold strong and firm to ideals that serve us, ideals that are positive, uplifting, all-inclusive, helpful, caring, light-filled, expansive, abundant, and loving (to name a few.) Resistances and limited thinking do not serve us; in fact, they keep us stuck in poverty, forever riding on the scarcity merry-go-round.

Though you have asked
for that which you desired,
there is so much more
that is awaiting to be given to you.

Lee Ching used to tell us to "spend ourselves into our abundance." He said that our abundance—and our scarcity—work like the kitchen faucet. When we open it up and let it flow freely, the water / abundance comes out in a steady stream. However, when we close off the faucet, the flow stops. Lee Ching recommended that we keep the faucet of our abundance wide open at all times and, in that way, we're sending the best possible message out to the Universe, a message that we whole-heartedly trust that whatever we spend will come back to us when we need it.

It took me almost twenty years to be able to completely trust in the idea of spending myself into my abundance. Every time I'd be in a store ready to buy something, a little voice in my head would say something like, "You can't afford it! You don't have enough money! The bills are coming due! It's too expensive!", etc. In all honesty, the voices scared the heck out of me at first, and I gave into their persuasiveness. But more recently—if I've really needed the item I'm looking at—I've gone ahead and bought it. And you know what? The money has always been replaced. Sure, sometimes it comes from totally unexpected sources. But if I really need it to pay my bills or for an emergency, the money is always there for me.

Our culture is steeped in scarcity. It's surprising, when we reflect upon it, how often we've been sitting around a coffee table with well-meaning friends when the subject of "hard times" has come up—and if we allowed ourself to buy into these "times are hard" suggestions, we'd have to live out the effects of our limiting thoughts. In a resource-based or love-based society, there's no room for scarcity or limitation because everyone will be sharing and giving to one another. That's the world we're preparing to step into. It's the world of our future. In the meantime, while the old ways still predominate here on Earth, the wisest thing we can do is withhold our agreement anytime someone is complaining about hard times. We can steer clear of thoughtless conversations while remaining positive and confident that all good things come to us when we trust and hold fast to our ideals.

The Highest Good is about gathering and holding your own power, not giving it away to somebody else.

Ideals Give Us Direction

Power and direction go hand in hand. BJ always emphasized that in order for us to be able to do anything, we needed to have both power and direction working on our behalf. If we didn't have the power, or enough energy, we could have all the direction in the world, but we wouldn't be able to do anything with it. We'd be like a ship floundering in the water, unable leave port because there's no fuel in the tanks. Direction without power, he said, is benign; it's useless.

On the other hand, power without direction is dangerous. To pursue our nautical analogy, it's like a ship going full speed ahead with a broken rudder, and no one at the helm. You never know where you'll end up. You could run into anything. BJ said that we needed to have both direction and power intact and working together; then we could use them to consciously create anything we choose. However, if we didn't have access to one or the other, we wouldn't be able to get where we want to go.

If we intend to create an ideal life for ourself, then we have to live as if that's the way it already is. We have to live it now. Our every word, our every act, our every expression must support life the way we truly want it to be. We can't compromise or be wishy-washy because that puts us back where we started. Even if it's not yet solid within us, we have to act as if it is. In this way, we introduce the blueprint for our highest ideals into the human matrix. We become ambassadors for the new reality. This is how we bring the dream of a better life, and as well as a better world, into our experience. We live as if our ideals have already manifested.

People who read our **Intenders Vision Alignment Project** often ask how we can hold to such lofty ideals. Most folks love the VAP visions, but occasionally someone will say they're too unrealistic, or they'll never happen. We don't listen to these naysayers, though, because we believe we can have it all, including the manifestation of our most outrageous, far-fetched ideals.

Indeed, if we don't have our ideals, we have nothing. Without them, we'd be blind, unable to see where we're headed. We need them like a ship's navigator needs a compass. They may not always manifest exactly as we intend them, but they start us out in the right direction. The test, for us, is to hold steadfast and firm to their manifestation and not give in to anyone who comes at us with doubts or skepticism. As long as we remember that the *Law of Attraction* is at work, it's simply a matter of trusting in the process. Here's an example of an ideal vision, compliments of our favorite guide.

While the mainstream would do its best to keep your attention on life's challenges, it serves you well to keep in mind the thousands of untold stories of kind, caring people who truly want to make things better for others, people who hold the ideal for doing good for their friends and neighbors.

It serves you to redouble your efforts to recognize and appreciate the vast majority of people who really care about their fellow travelers: the driver who slows down and lets you pull out in front of her; the man who goes out of his way to open the door for a stranger; the off-duty nurse who peeks her head into the hospital room door for no other reason than to bring a bit of cheer to an ailing child; the firemen and policewomen who risk their lives daily so others may live; the nameless giver who shares a few dollars with the homeless person on the street corner.

Furthermore, it serves you to acknowledge the teachers, the doctors and nurses, the construction workers, the shopkeepers, the miners, the mechanics, the farmers, as well as the hard-working people who rise early and drive, often long distances, so that you can enjoy all the services and products you've become accustomed to having. Learn to dwell only on the good that people do for each other everyday. In this way, you make the highest and best use of your attention and intention. Indeed, whatever you're putting your attention and intention on is what you're becoming.

Lee Ching

**When you give your attention
to that which is good,
you just make more of it.**

{Remember}
Optimism gives us success

The world needs more optimists. Optimistic people are positive people. They don't shy away in the face of life's adverse circumstances. Instead, they have a knowing that everything will turn out all right. They're the kind of people you like to hang around because they're typically happier than other people. They'll cheer you up when you're troubled and feeling like the rest of the world is against you. And, most of all, they'll roll up their sleeves and help get you started off on the right foot when you're going through troubling times.

One of the best things we can do for ourself is to be as positive as possible, as much of the time as possible. Whether we know it or not, when we hold an optimistic outlook on life, we're putting the *Law of Attraction* to its highest and best use. As we think things will be okay, then things turn out okay. This is one of the great secrets of life: that to think positive thoughts is to bring positive experiences into our life.

Stop talking about the worst that can happen,
and start talking about the best that can happen.

It's a teacher's job to uplift those who come to her for advice. One day not too long ago, I was fortunate to sit in on a session with my friends, Betsy and Sandy. Sandy had come to Betsy for help because she knew Betsy was a happy person. They chatted about little things for a while, then Sandy began complaining about several problems she was having. Her bank account was near empty; her job was unfulfilling; her car just broke down and needed repairs, etc.

As I sat there, I felt an urge to commiserate with Sandy because she was so sad about her circumstances. But Betsy never wavered from her optimism. She held a positive outlook, no matter what Sandy was saying. When Sandy complained about money, Betsy told her that unexpected money was on the way to her (how Betsy knew this, I don't know, but it turned out to be true). When Sandy complained about her job, Betsy talked to her about it and made a few suggestions that would make Sandy's work go more smoothly. When Sandy mentioned her vehicle issues, Betsy recommended an honest mechanic friend who lived down the street.

No matter what Sandy said, Betsy invariably had a helpful solution. It was a beautiful sight to see, and I felt lucky to be a bystander to their conversation. The best thing about the whole situation was that when Sandy got up to leave, the lines in her face had gone away. She was visibly happier as she hugged Betsy goodbye. It was clear that some of Betsy's optimism had rubbed off on her. In fact, I'm sure that Sandy's

problems would lessen or go away entirely now that
she had a more positive outlook on it all.

It's good to help others who need it;
just be sure not to get caught up in their stuff.

Commiseration works against us, and
optimism works on our behalf. Always see the
bright side, and life will be brighter, gifts will be
given, and the way to happiness will be smoother
in all your endeavors. When others say it can't be
done, you say it can. When others are beset with
life's challenges, you show them the way out of
their challenges. One of the great joys in life is
when someone you've helped comes back to you
a few days or weeks later and thanks you because
your help changed their life. In that moment,
you'll know that they're in a more positive place
now, and they're more apt to stay uplifted from
then on.

Let nothing come between you and your joy.

Moderation Refreshes Us

It's definitely in our highest and best good to understand and apply the *Law of Diminishing Returns*. In fact, if this little known law were to be taught to us from childhood on, our lives would be much happier, much healthier, and we'd be better equipped to face the crises of life.

Briefly put, this law says that when we continue to do anything for too long, we run the risk of problems coming our way. For example, we can eat one chocolate bonbon, and it's good; and we can usually eat two or three chocolate bonbons, and it's still okay. But after eight or nine bonbons, we have to get away from them for a while, so they can digest. Then, we can come back later and enjoy eating bonbons again.

The interesting thing about the *Law of Diminishing Returns* is that it not only applies to bonbons; it applies to everything we do. It explains why things fall apart in our lives, because when we go on too long with anything—from our jobs, our relationships, our favorite foods, our pills and powders, our habits of all kinds—we'll need to get away from them for awhile, so we can come back renewed and continue on with what we were doing.

One of the most common misuses of the Law of Diminishing Returns happens in our relationships. I have acquaintances, Barry and Sue, who bicker and argue to the point when one of them eventually storms out of the house and drives off to parts unknown for anywhere from a few hours to a few days. They say they love each other, but sometimes it's hard to see.

One day, Barry came over complaining about Sue's untidyness, and her keeping him waiting all the time, and her disinterest in his work, and so on. Clearly, he needed to learn about the Law of Diminishing Returns and get away for a while. But when I explained it to him, he dismissed it without any further interest. He didn't understand that he needed to take a break long enough to be able to come back renewed and loving again.

A couple of days later, Sue came over with a similar list of complaints about Barry. When she'd finished ranting, I told her the same thing I'd told him—that they needed to know when to get away from one another for a short time so their relationship could be refreshed. I even mentioned that if they stayed in close proximity with each other for too long, they'd be putting their relationship at risk.

Well, Sue got it. She didn't want to lose her relationship with a man she loved deeply, just because they didn't know when to be apart. That afternoon, she went home, talked to Barry, and they made a friendly decision to take a short break from each other. Barry went on a golfing trip with his buddies, and Sue went to visit her sister in Utah for a few days.

I saw them a week later, and I couldn't help but notice how lovey-dovey they were after their short time apart. I was so happy for them because they'd learned one of the great lessons of life: that we have to deliberately get away from the things we love every-so-often in order to keep them fresh in our lives.

Because we don't always notice when things have gone on too long, and we don't apply the *Law of Diminishing Returns* to our habitual behavior, the people and things we love most are kept in perpetual jeopardy of falling apart. However, when we become aware enough to be able to notice the exact moment when we've gone on too long—and we *consciously* halt our immoderations long enough to renew ourself—then we can avoid any problems that may arise. In short, those who know when to get away from their job, their partner, or their immoderate consumption of chocolate bonbons will have a happier, more comfortable ride through life than those who don't know when to stop and take a break.

I have other friends, Jake and Patty, who get along so well that it astounds me. They're perpetually happy with each other. One day, Jake and I were having coffee, and I asked him what the secret was to their happiness.

"Tony, early on in our marriage, I began to notice that there were a couple of times every month when things around the house started getting a little edgy. Either she'd get a bit grumpy, or I would. That's when I'd decide to go fishing. I didn't let things go past the point where we'd have an argument."

I asked him how Patty felt about him dropping everything else and going fishing at a moment's notice, "Oh, she doesn't like it at first," he said, "because she tends to be clingy and not wanting me to leave. But I go fishing anyway, and you know what? It doesn't take long after I'm gone that she's got the music on loud, and she's dancing wildly around the living room, *happy to have some time to herself!"*

"So, that's your recipe for a happy marriage?" I asked him.

"It works for us," he replied. "If more people knew when to take a short break from one another, there'd be a whole lot less marriage failures and breakups in this world. People would be happier and stay together longer, just because they're making good use of the Law of Diminishing Returns."

**To be in balance,
cultivate moderation in all things.**

{Remember}
Communication Connects Us

Most of my adult life has been dedicated to helping people set up small, independent Intenders Circles. Those of us in our original Intenders Circle never intended to connect the circles together—but we loved sharing our beautiful model for creating a local community of self-empowered people who are interested in consciously manifesting their desires by making intentions together. As a result, the number of circles grew beyond our wildest dreams, but it didn't all go without a hitch. If you've ever been in a community, you know that it has to have some well thought-out parameters around how the members communicate with one another. What we found is that the most successful communities—the ones that last the longest and serve their members the best—are the ones where everyone is allowed equal time to express themself. Communities where one person does all the talking while everyone else listens only work well in teaching situations. But communities are not all devoted to teaching. Many exist in order to create an environment in which each person can share their ideas and intentions, as well as come together socially with their friends and neighbors.

A circle presents one of the best models for communicating in community. The ancients, as well as most native tribes, knew this and gathered in circles around campfires to share their wisdom and their stories. They knew that everyone has equal access to everyone else in a circle, and that people cannot be allowed to take all the energy generated in the circle unto themselves. They understood the energy dynamics of the circle and protected its integrity for the Highest Good of the whole. In this way, they created equality and Oneness in their community.

Today's communities often struggle to accomplish what the ancients took for granted. Community groups today tend to fall into the trap of one person taking all of the group's energy for themself. These people keep talking long past the point of communicating; indeed, they go on and on, not realizing that they're doing more harm than good to their friends. It's like they get so wrapped up in the energy of the group that they forget their original purpose, which is to communicate ideas that lead to an understanding and, ultimately, *to a feeling*.

I was in an Intenders Circle in Michigan recently with about 40 enthusiastic, newfound friends. Before we began, I gently requested that we each keep our intention and gratitude sharing down to about 3 minutes or less. Otherwise, I explained, we'd be there until midnight. They all happily agreed, and I must tell you that it was a delightful circle with everyone expressing themself without anyone going on too long —until we reached the last lady to take her turn. She started sharing right away, but what she was saying was drama-driven and had nothing to do with her intentions or gratitudes. As sweet as she was, she went on and on, long past the three minute limit.

While she rambled on, I looked around the large circle and noticed that everyone was tired and wanted to get to the closing Oneness exercise. I also felt that they'd seen her do something like this before. So, when she took a quick breath, I gently said, "Helen, what are your intentions?" and she unexpectedly snapped at me. "I'm talking!" she said, and it felt like the air had just been sucked out of the room. Everyone was glad I interrupted her, but they were taken aback by her response. Fortunately, within about 30 seconds, she seemed to realize what she was doing and finished up, never really having stated her intentions. As you can imagine, the whole group let out a subtle sigh, thankful that I'd stopped her from going on any longer ... whereupon I quickly stood up, started the toning, sending us all into the most beautiful state of Oneness imaginable.

Communication is an art. It has to do with one person having an idea in his head with the intent of passing that idea onto another. When this happens, it's a beautiful thing. Anything else is just talking, and that's okay, but it has little to do with communicating. People who are *consciously* intending to pass information onto another know that all thoughts lead to a feeling, and until that thought is transferred into another's mind, and the feeling has arisen, communication has not truly happened. By the same token, they know that when the person who is being communicated to has an "AHA!" moment, and experiences an accompanying feeling, true communication has occurred.

> *You don't really have it,*
> *unless you can give it away.*

And this brings us back to our circle. A good communicator or leader knows when to be still. She knows that there are specific times in her presentation when, if she continues to say one more word, she will sabotage everything she has said up to that point. She will lose the opportunity to communicate, and lose the feeling she could have created in her listener. It's like a comedian on stage who doesn't know the exact moment when to stop talking and let his audience have a good laugh. If he prattles on, unwilling to be still and let his punch lines settle in, the people won't come back to see him anymore. It's the same in business organizations, religious and spiritual groups, and any gatherings where people come together to share ideas. If one person doesn't know when to stop talking, it hurts the whole group.

A good group leader will also know how the flow of the circle or gathering should go. Oftentimes she'll set a time limit for sharing (depending on the size of the group), or she will suggest that they "play tag", where the one who just finished sharing "tags" anyone else in the group. Or she'll pass a feather or a talking stick, like the Native Americans do. These models keep the flow of the gathering going so that everyone in the community has the opportunity to express himself. They help to keep anyone from holding the entire group hostage with his will and commandeering the energy of group all to himself. Both in groups and in private conversations, a conscious leader knows how to keep the flow going, and she also knows when to gently interrupt anyone who goes on talking too long.

Taking another's energy away not only happens in group settings, it's also quite common in one-on-one conversations. I have a good friend, William, who doesn't know when to be quiet. We'll be talking about something and, at first, our conversion proceeds nicely with each of us giving equal time to the other in order to share our ideas. But typically, within a few minutes, he's leaning forward into my space, raising his voice, and not letting me get a word in edgewise. He goes on and on, to the point where I begin to feel my energy being drained, and if I try to stop him or express my viewpoint, he gets even louder and talks even faster.

I'll bet you know people like this. Once they get up a head of steam, it's like they've forgotten you're even there. They're holding you with their will, and often don't even know it because they're so enveloped in the momentum of it all that they can't seem to stop. The only problem is that communication has stopped. Any ideas they had in their head are no longer being integrated into my mine because I'm just wanting to get away and keep from being dumped on any further.

Nowadays, I politely interrupt and excuse myself as quickly as possible. Sometimes this upsets William, especially when he's on a roll, however I've realized that even though he won't respect my boundaries, I

164

have to respect them for myself. I've told him about his behavior several times, and he still hasn't changed his willful ways. In the meantime, I don't visit with him as often as I used to because I just don't want my energy taken away. I need it for myself.

When someone is going on about their drama, you can suggest that they make an intention around it—and very soon, the drama will be gone because the intention they made has manifested for them.

{Remember}
Adversity Corrects Us

People often ask how it could possibly be in our Highest Good if we've been in an accident or experienced some unexpected adversity? In these instances, something in our life had to be out of alignment that was in need of correction. Perhaps we were so far removed from fulfilling our calling in life that drastic action was needed in order for us to be able to return to the purpose for which we came to this beautiful planet.

Our challenges are there
in order to lead us to a greater awareness.

We see this happen all the time. People intend to fulfill a certain task or goal, and then something in our acquisitive culture distracts them and pulls them away from their original course. Perhaps greed, or pride, or envy enticed them with great pleasures and treasures. Fortunately, the Highest Good is always at work behind the scenes, waiting for the day when they intend to come back into alignment with it. If they aren't paying attention or are too busy to notice, then the Highest Good may take stronger measures, including accidents or life-threatening circumstances in order to help them correct their course. These measures are always in exact accordance with the amount of change that is needed. No one ever suffers one minute longer than they need to. For some, it may take months or years, while, for others, correction can come in an instant. Our adversity lasts only for as long as it takes for us come back into balance with our Highest Good.

All my life I've wanted things. When I was growing up, like all kids, I wanted toys and bicycles and erector sets. I wanted gadgets like my friends had. I wanted more of everything. As I grew older, though, the symbols of my wanting changed, but the practical function remained the same: I was a wanter. Only now, my wants had expanded. I wanted travel and relationships with others. I wanted excitement and exotic places. I wanted it all.

The first time I recall wanting happened when I was about four years old. My parents and I had just finished eating dinner at the local Walgreens (back when they had a cafeteria). As we stood in line at the cash register waiting to pay our bill, I caught sight of a bright, red Swiss army knife on the rack beside the check-out counter. Within seconds, I was throwing a giant tantrum right there in the check-out aisle. I screamed and cried and wallowed around the tile floor, refusing to move another inch until my daddy bought me the knife.

Seeing that my tantrum wasn't letting up, and embarrassed by my behavior, he reluctantly agreed and, against my mom's reservations, he bought me the red knife. I was never so happy in all my life! But it wasn't another minute before blood was streaming down my hand, and I was crying again—this time, not from my wanting, but from the big, gushing slice across my left index finger. It was a lesson I would repeat in many different ways throughout my life, although this first instance at Walgreens became a strong reminder of the risks I take when I go against the Highest Good. Both my mom and dad had tried to talk me out of getting the knife, but my wanting was so strong that it overpowered any of their better judgments.

Sometimes, it seems, we have to learn our lessons the hard way, through painful injuries, illnesses, or uncomfortable circumstances. The Highest Good, however, would have us avoid our suffering by signaling us to let go (or, at least, be willing to let go) of our wanting. Indeed, we discover our greatest joy when we've finally detached from our wants and allowed the Highest Good to show us what's next.

It's taken me a lifetime to learn this lesson. Perhaps I could've figured it out back when I cut my finger with the shiny red knife at Walgreens. I'm not sure that that's the way life works, though. The older I get, the more I've come to realize that life is a growth process, and that sometimes our egos are so powerful, and life is so fun, that we have to go through our trials before *we finally let go and let the Highest Good take over.*

The Highest Good
is communicating to you as best it can.
The Highest Good is guiding you
to your awakening.

The Highest Good sets up lessons for us that are consciously designed to bring us back on course, a course we set for ourselves before we came into this lifetime, a course that ultimately leads back to our peace and our joy. In fact, the Highest Good is always directing us toward our greatest fulfillment; it's us, with our own *"wanting"* ways, that cause all of our pain and adversity. The correction that needs to be made is not by the Highest Good; it needs to be made by us. We wander off and the Highest Good is constantly doing whatever is necessary to bring us back to love.

The Highest Good has the most beautiful plans
for both you and the world.
You just have to open up to it.

Non-Violence Heals Us

Is what I'm doing serving me and my fellow travelers?
This question is foremost in our minds whenever
we're talking with anyone else, and we ask it
often. We also ask ourselves if what we're doing is
apt to cause someone else harm? Or, is the work
we're doing designed to contribute to another's
pain or suffering? If so, it's highly unlikely that
the Highest Good is being served, and it might be
time for us to reevaluate our activities. It's a *"do
unto others"* world whether we know it or not, and
those who do not respect the relationship between
their sowing/causes and their reaping/effects set
themselves up to pay a price they may not see
coming.

> *Harming another will never give you
> the results you're looking for.
> In point of fact, it will only makes things worse.*

The wisdom of *"First do no harm"* is a sure guide
for keeping us aligned with the Highest Good. If
what you're doing unto others is meant to harm

them, perhaps you might want to find something else to do with your time, something that wouldn't come back to bite you in the long run, something you'd want to be doing unto yourself.

Everything gets better for you as you learn to honor, support and nurture all of life—while everything gets worse, both individually and collectively, when you do anything to bring harm to another. If you bought into the idea that serving your country by killing others is better than serving the poor or the sick people down the block, then perhaps you might want to reevaluate your thinking. There is no shortage of people to love, and no shortage of people to hate and kill. The decision is up to you. Just be sure to make your choice based on your own ideals, not someone else's.

Lee Ching

Mainstream Miscreation #6 ~ Opposition
How We Create Enemies
(and how we can transmute them.)

If someone comes along and tells you that a bunch of strange people from across the water are out to get you, would you automatically believe them and agree? Would you make an enemy of the distant people, or would you first question the motivations and truthfulness of the person who is warning you? This is the conundrum facing many people in our world today. Do you believe others are your enemies just because someone else tells you so? Or do you question?

Our beautiful young men and women put their lives on the line on the world's battlefields everyday because they trust in what those who've created their enemies tell them. They honestly believe that someone is out to harm them or take away their comfortable lifestyle, so they fight and die in the name of country and keeping things safe at home. But is this true—and how many bullets flying or bombs dropping must we endure before we begin to question who our enemy really is?

If you're holding a defensive position,
it's because you're thinking
that someone is out to attack you.
Like all thoughts,
the thought of being attacked
—if you place enough attention on it—
will manifest itself into your daily experience.

Isn't it time we asked ourselves if the on-going creation of enemies and wars is what we really want for ourselves? Is it for our Highest Good? In truth, anyone who supports an institution dedicated to killing other people is a killer in his own right. Compassionate and caring people cannot sit idly by and claim allegiance to any country, business, or regime if that regime openly advocates the killing of even one individual. We either stand for killing and war, or we don't. There's no middle ground, and no burying our heads in the sand.

So, how do we line up with the Highest Good in our daily life? We disavow harming, and we honor all life. We remain at peace amid all the saber-rattling and chaos, and we steadfastly choose non-violence. We choose life, not only for ourselves, but for all our fellowmen, women, and children—including the people we previously thought were "the bad guys." Now we see "the bad guys" in a new light, realizing that oftentimes they are members of our soul family who have agreed to come into our life to play the role of our opponent in order to show us our own unconscious aggressive tendencies? Once we learn to forgive them, instead of opposing them, we open the way for both of us to be free. Indeed, when we stand firm and tall for life, all life—including our former enemies' lives—we engage the miraculous machinery of the Highest Good to work on our behalf. We step aside from all the violence and step into being guided, guarded, protected, and provided for by the Highest Good.

You'll always be shown the right direction.
You just have to trust in it.
You'll go, "Oh, if I go this way,
it leads to more suffering...
and if I go that way,
everything will work out
much better for everyone!"

In our worldly affairs, one of the next best steps we can take is to anchor peace onto this Earth. But first we need to see that what's stopping us from bringing peace forth is our own unwillingness to create peace within. Indeed, we cannot expect our neighbor or our supposed enemies to be peaceful if we do not first have the peace that comes from forgiveness in ourselves. Peace comes first in our mind, and then in our heart, and then it can flow outward from there to help others find peace within themselves. We can learn to forgive our supposed enemies, or we can hate and kill them. Hate and killing will only continue to harm us and our fellowmen and women. However, when we forgive those who are opposing us, then both of us are benefited and blessed. Hate keeps us apart, while forgiveness bring us back together for our Highest Good.

Once these ideas are fully understood, we will see, ever-so-clearly, that there are no "bad guys" and that our aggressive ways are no longer serving us. We will see that peace, true peace, is the only avenue that furthers us, all of us, even those who advocate war. We'll see that our worst fears go away the minute peace breaks out, and we'll breathe much easier as we discover that we're able to go about our days and nights freely and fully from that moment on.

The world you live in is splitting apart.
The old selfish ways are collapsing,
and at the same time,
the new spiritual ways are emerging,
heralding a better life for all.

It's for you to bring peace to Earth by intending it, envisioning it, feeling it in advance, and being grateful for it in advance—and in doing, so you set the anchor of peace one layer deeper into the hearts and minds of all mankind. Just imagine it. Peace has broken out! Every move you make is done in the knowing that you can fulfill your life's calling to full completion; everyone you talk to is excited again now that they can move forward without being interrupted by those with violent intent; everywhere you look, people are moving about, happy and free now that you're all living in peace. Isn't it worth it to support a peace that offers so much? Isn't it in your Highest Good that you stop judging your supposed enemies, forgive them, and begin to work on behalf of peace now?

Anchoring peace by forgiving your enemies: unquestionably, that's your next worldly step ... but it doesn't happen out in the world. It all happens in your mind.

Lee Ching

**Peace is not just a word. It is a way of being—
and when you experience it within yourself,
you are assisting others in the world
to have that peace as well.**

It's All In Present Time

I don't know about you, but I've spent a large portion of my life daydreaming about the past and the future. I really didn't know what the "*Now*" was all about until I experienced it. I thought it would be similar to all my other daily experiences, but it definitely was not. The present moment shines with an intensity of awareness that is so profound that it makes our daydreaming seem small and inconsequential in comparison.

At this time in our history, we're moving from an awareness seemingly locked within the worlds of past and future to the world of here and now. But first, we'll need to let go of the worlds of past and future, worlds that are very easy to get hung up in. For when we're able to let go of these illusionary mental constructs, our true identity is revealed to us, along with our Divine direction. We discover a heightened state of awareness. We come face to face with our Higher Self.

We can access the present moment by being mindful or by meditating, but sometimes it takes an illness, or a loss, or a shock in our lives to bring us into the Now. I was driving on I-40 through western Oklahoma on the last leg of last year's tour when one of the worst rainstorms I'd ever encountered suddenly pelted my car. I was dog-tired and just wanted to get home as quickly as possible, but the rain was coming down so hard that I knew I had to get off the road to safety somehow. Huge trucks whizzed by; I truly couldn't see a thing.

Out in the middle of nowhere, with no visibility whatsoever, I had to focus like never before. Nothing else mattered except what was happening right in front of me. All daydreams of past and future were set aside, as I intended that I find a pull-off.

I slowed down to a crawl on the freeway, not knowing if someone was going to plow into me from behind—and it was then that two things happened simultaneously. First, the rest of the world melted away, as my attention heightened to a new level. Only the present moment existed; there was only me and the road and the rain. And second, a huge semi flew by on my left splashing a spray of water across my entire windshield. When it cleared, from out of the corner of my eye, I caught sight of a small, blue, rectangular road sign through my passenger side window. To this day, I don't know what it said, however, just past it, the edge of the road seemed to veer to the right. Without being able to see more than five feet in front of me, I slowly pulled off the freeway onto the side of the road, not knowing where it would take me. To my great relief, a traveler's rest stop appeared directly ahead. I turned in, shut off the engine, and sat there in a state of joy. I'll never forget it. It was as if the whole world had come alive in those intense moments, and the angels had steered me to safety.

If you're on a path for your Highest Good, things will eventually smooth out and open up. When you discover it, it just takes you along, like a river, into the Now.

When chaos is the order of the day, you are given the greatest of opportunities to learn and evolve. As you are pushed to your limits on all levels of life, an intensity wells up within you that can be used to catapult you to the next realm. If you can keep from lashing out negatively in blame of others, that intensity will lift you up to a higher experience.

These times of great chaos offer you the very best environment in which to find the love, the joy, and *the peace that is within you. For when you rise up and out of the prevailing mainstream fear, you come face to face with the higher attributes that have been hidden within you all along. The intense conditions around you have forced you to look inside, to go deeper, and to let go. Indeed, it's in the forgiving and letting go of the old that the new is born. It's in the thick of chaos that love rises to the surface. It's in the depths of despair that the Highest Good offers its greatest rewards.*

Lee Ching

The present moment is our window into knowing who we are. When we can look upon anything in our sphere of vision without our attention wavering, we'll be delivered into a higher experience in direct proportion to how mindful we are. BJ used to say to pick any spot in space and hold our attention on it for as long as we can. He called it *"strengthening our attention muscle,"* and said that when we got good at it, it would transport us into parts of ourself that we didn't know existed. He said that our attention span is all-important to us, and we can lengthen and strengthen it until nothing comes between us and our glory.

{Remember}
It's All In Perfect Order

Sometimes it's difficult to imagine that everything going on in our world and in our lives is for the Highest Good, but it's true. Each event, each joy, each sorrow, each pleasure, each pain, each war, each time of peace, each birth, and each death is just as it should be. Nothing is out of place. Never is one distanced from the Highest Good in the least, although from our worldly, judgmental perspective, it may seem like it at times. Even when we're suffering or feeling lost, the Highest Good is there, guiding us ever-so-surely toward our next step in life

For four years I was stranded in a remote village in the mountains of the Northern Philippines. Fortunately, during this time, I was able to receive your Vision Newsletter by email and I was deeply inspired by it. Also, even more fortunately, the folks of the village accepted me for one of them and I was able to learn much of their wisdom. My neighbors were one of the few unconquered indigenous peoples on the planet—the Igorots. Their ancestral way of life still

181

thrives in abundant harmony with the cycles of life.

One problem that I encountered was what to do with my plastic waste in the community. There was nowhere for it to go. Inspired by Igorot wisdom (and from your newsletter!), we developed a technology for transforming our polluting plastic into building blocks for our gardens—using bottles. This started at my house, then spread to the school. This 'Vision Ecobrick' technology has since taken off from our village to others. It is now implemented in an opensource curriculum guide that went out this past year to over 200,000 students. Just as you invite visions, our curriculum guide helps teachers invite each student to en-vision their community in harmony with the environment and to make ecobricks.

So, of course, since we're inviting visions from our students, I had to write one too. I wrote mine in story format to embrace both past and future with the vision. I would like to share it with you and your readers (the whole guide can be found at www.ecobricks.org). I am grateful for your example of inspiring and sharing visions. Please know that you're inspiring others across the planet! This year we have the go-ahead from the very highest level of the Filipino government to implement visioning nationwide to approximately

18 million students. Please keep us in your prayers as we undertake this massive vision-empowering opportunity.

— — —

Not so long ago, in the land right here, our Ancestors lived in harmony with the plants and animals around them. Their homes, clothes, food, and community were like melodies that danced to the songs of Nature's Cycles. Our Great-great-great-grandparents grew food so healthy that they danced all through their long and lively lifetimes. Our Great-great-grandparents had to work hard, but it was rewarding work that saw their family and community blossom like the flowers and fruits in their gardens. Nothing was wasted. Everything they used was returned to the Circles of Life.

As our Great-Grandparents prospered, they became excited at the new things they could make, buy, and trade. They lovingly sought to make the lives of their children easier with new inventions, substances, and stuff. But in their passion, our Grandparents forgot how these new things would fit back into the world around us. Waste arrived. And it began to pile up. Sickness and disease followed closely behind.

Afraid for the future, our Grandparents locked the animals and plants in mass cages, mono-fields, and plastic packages. There was more food—but it seemed to make people sick. And there was even more waste. Our parents were even more concerned for their children—for us. They worked even harder to solve the problems. But try as they might, the waste piled ever higher.

Almost forgotten, the gentle melodies of our ancestors sung back to us across the generations. And WE could hear it. We realized, we remembered, that we are part of nature's song, just as the flowers, the fields, the trees—and the trash. The song included it also—what we had thought was waste was but new notes for our ears. Bottles and plastics and cellophane were not useless—they were marvelous materials to be segregated, saved, and sung into new songs never before heard!

Together, we began to work with our parents and grandparents to transform our problems into solutions. Together, we began to bend dead-end, product-to-pollution lines back into circles of use and re-use. It was a lot of work, and it was even more fun. Our gray communities began to return to green, the plants and animals frolicked freely, and our children were happier than ever before as they played in the rivers, fields, and forests.

Never before had the planet sung so sweetly, for once again—this time with deep intention—our homes, ways, and lives were melodies in harmony with the song and cycles of life.

Russell Maier

Even though we may not always start off in the right direction, when we trust in the Highest Good, we'll be shown what to do next. As long as we're willing to keep moving forward —as Russell and the Filipinos have done—and wait attentively for our goals and intentions to manifest, we'll be rewarded in ways we may never have anticipated.

Your next step is revealed to you in each moment, with each new experience that comes your way. You needn't go out and search for it; it will find you. The only variable lies in your alertness, in your ability to notice it when gifts are being presented to you. Indeed, when you're able to make the most of the opportunities that come your way, your next step in life is always revealed to you.

Evolution is not to be forced, but to be allowed to

happen at its own pace. As you permit things to arrive of their own volition, you avoid all of the striving and stressing you see so many others dealing with. You no longer worry about what's next because you know that the perfect event will show itself to you at the perfect time. Everything unfolds like a flower that bursts forth from its bud in the mid-morning summer sun.

The days of your emotional rollercoaster rides will be over as soon as you let go and allow things to come of their own accord. When you can do this, the first thing you'll discover is that "waiting" has become your friend. For it's in the waiting that true serenity settles into your days and nights. You are serene, alertly waiting for your next step in life to show itself. And it surely will, in the same measure that you are willing to receive it.

Lee Ching

**You needn't strive for everything.
Life is a journey
and the experiences
needed for your learning and your growth
will come up in the course of life itself—
if you let them.**

Love Is All Around Us

Love, God, Truth, Source, Heavenly Father, Holy Spirit, All That Is, Oneness, Great Spirit, Allah, Creator, Highest Good. These are some of the names for the same thing. But, let's not get hung up on the words at this point. Instead, let's go straight to the substance that breathes life into these sacred names.

All of our great religious and spiritual teachings bid us to go directly to God, to call Him forth, to invoke Him through prayer, affirmation, or intention. This is how we get results. We go straight to the Source and ask for what we want. Of course, it's alright to use intermediaries—angels, ascended masters, invisible guides, and helpers—in order to approach God, and we do this all the time. In fact, we highly recommend it because, when we approach God through Jesus Christ or an archangel, it's often easier to reach the feeling that accompanies the God Source. Indeed, every angel and master has his/her own distinct flavor or feeling to be savored, and it's this feeling that can open the way to a higher spiritual experience.

Our world is teeming with life, and most of it is invisible. We don't often question the invisibility of the air we breathe, the emotions we feel, the thoughts we think, the TV waves or cell phone frequencies that are constantly surrounding us, but we still tend to discount the fact that invisible living beings are surrounding us, as well. Those who are sharpening their intuitive senses, however, are finding that communication with invisible beings is fast becoming a way of life. We're finding that we can tap into them and receive their messages anytime we like. All we need to do is ask—and learn to discern.

Beings from other realms
can really help us learn
because they're not so entrapped
in the everyday world.

When we first begin to communicate with invisible beings, we find that some of them are in alignment with the Highest Good, and some of them are definitely not. Until we're able to tell the difference and to call forth only those who care about our best interests, we'll be well served to pay closer attention to the voices in our head and to our emotions. For those are the places where contact with invisible beings is to be found: in our mind and in the center of our solar plexus. Accordingly, we can discern by checking in with how we feel and what we're thinking to see if the information being imparted to us from the unseen worlds is helpful to us or not. On an emotional level, we can ask ourselves: *"Does this feel good to me?" "Is there an expanded or a restricted feeling in my solar plexus?" "Is this love or fear I'm feeling?"* Likewise, we can do the same thing with the thoughts we're thinking, and find out how they're affecting us, by asking ourself, *"Is the thought that's just arisen serving me?" "Will it bring me happiness?" "If it manifests, will I like the outcome of it, or not?"*

The answers to these questions will tell us whether the guidance we're receiving from the invisible realms is meant to help us or rob us of our precious energy. We must be very truthful with ourselves in discerning the answers to these questions because many in the unseen are extremely deceptive. We must be constantly on the lookout, for many in the invisible realms are adept at getting us all riled up, so they can feed

off of our negative emotional responses. They
literally nourish themselves off of our fear and
anger, and it is up to us to stop feeding them. It is
up to us to keep our attention only on the voices
and feelings that are loving and forgiving.

*There comes a point when we only allow
the Highest Good to come through.*

We Intenders have found a way to insure that
only loving invisibles are coming through us, and
we have outlined this method in several of our
previous books. It has to do with setting our course
for what we want to manifest. In calling forth
positive unseen helpers, like Jesus, the ascended
masters, the angels and so forth, we make a
particular intention or prayer that guarantees that
we're heading in a loving direction. We know that
*what we say is precisely what we'll get, and so who we
call forth is who will show up.* Therefore, if we don't
take a moment to invoke positive invisible beings,
then any slippery invisible being can show up,
and we can fall into doing its bidding. But when
we call forth only those who stand for the Highest
Good, those are the only ones who can and will

come forth to help us. It's the law.

Here's the way we do it (and feel free to use this method as your own). We take a couple of deep breaths, quiet our mind for a moment, and then say: *"I intend that I am held in the highest light imaginable; that everything needing to be known is known here today; that all of my thoughts and words are clear, precise, uplifting, helpful for others, and enjoyable for me; I intend that I am guided, guarded, protected, and provided for throughout this entire experience; and that everything I think and say and feel and do here serves the Highest and Best Good of the Universe, myself, and everyone concerned. So be it and so it is. It is done!"*

It's as simple as that and, when we're undistracted, it always works for us. After that, all we have to do is be open to receive the guidance that comes into our mind, along with the sweet feeling that accompanies the arrival of our loving, unseen friends.

Every single one of us
is capable of bringing through our Higher Self.

The great masters have already been where we are going, and they're unaffected by physical limitations. They control their bodies and are able to shift into other shapes. Jesus rose from the dead; St. Germaine never aged; Lee Ching lived 170 years and left of his own accord; Gurdjieff and Don Juan rearranged their appearances at will. The list is endless.

The day will come when we all have the ability to change our appearance, to live longer, to create optimal health for ourselves, and more. From our earliest childhood, we've been taught to believe that these abilities are unavailable to us. But now, as the transition to the new ways is upon us, new opportunities and potentials become more available. We're becoming more than we were before....

As we let go of our old attachments and our identifications with our bodies and our earthly programming, we find that our Spirit blossoms and brings new possibilities. Indeed, our intentions play a key role in all of this. No master ever shifted anything without intending it first.

**Call forth your guides and masters within,
for that is where you will find them:
within you.**

We're More Than We Think We Are

On the farm, BJ was always pushing my buttons (with my consent), and, whenever I was hung up on a thinking pattern that was programmed into me when I was young, he would say something to provoke a response, so I would clearly see my old ways of thinking and begin to rise above them. One day, not long after we met, we were building terraces on my steep land on the west side of Moana Loa. As we were raking the dirt toward the edge of the first terrace and casually chatting about the art of fine-tuning our work, BJ abruptly turned to me and said, "Tony, don't you want to wake up?"

Right away, I felt my stomach churn. He'd just triggered something in me, and I wasn't even sure what it was. "I didn't know I was asleep," I replied.

He set his rake aside and looked at me disapprovingly. "Well, you most certainly are asleep," he said. "You don't even know who you are, or what you're doing here."

I felt my anger starting to surface, but at the same time, I was curious. "You just lost me," I said, not realizing that his next words would change my life.

"You think that you're Tony Burroughs," he said, "but those are just a couple of words your parents made up. They're not you, are they?"

I stopped raking and gave him my full attention.

"You think that you're your story, your memories, your past experiences, but if you look around, you'll see that they're not here now. They're just a series of events in your mind that you keep telling yourself about yourself. They're in the past. They're a dream that keeps you from experiencing the fullness of who you really are in the moment. You can be anybody you want to be, and you can tell any story about yourself that you like. There's no law that says you have to think who you are has anything to do with your story. You're not your past experiences."

Wow! This was blowing my mind! Nobody had ever talked like this to me before. As unsettling as it was, I felt excited. If I wasn't my name or my story, then who was I?

As if to know what I was thinking, BJ paused and let me ponder his words for a few moments, then he went on, "You think you're an avocado farmer; you think you're an American; you think you are your body. But these things that you identify with are definitely not you. You're much, much more than these beliefs

194

you have about yourself. They're part of the dream. They're what's keeping you asleep."

At the time, I was confused. I didn't know what to think. Later on, I remember hiking up the mountain and mulling his words over in greater detail. Who am I if I'm not my name, or my story, or my body? Like a flash, it hit me! I'm the being who lives inside this body! I'm the Spirit Essence who animates and brings everything I experience to light and to life! I can think what I want, and I can be whoever I want. I don't have to stay wedded to what someone else has told me about myself ... I am more. I was waking up.

To the extent that we believe what others have told us about ourselves, we remain in the dream. Likewise, as we attach ourselves to the people, places, possessions, and objects, as well as the thought patterns and beliefs of this world, we keep ourselves asleep to the vastness of who we really are. We must let go—*or at least be willing to let go*—of our worldly attachments and identifications. It's not in our Highest Good to keep believing and holding onto them indefinitely. Our Highest Good calls upon us to awaken from these dreams, to reach out in these most exciting of times, and to expand into the highest version of ourself.

It's amazing that our consciousness
even fits into our body.

You misrepresent yourselves. Almost every time
you use the word "I", it's not who you really are. For
in truth, at your core, you are the Spirit, the Essence,
who resides for the time being in your body. You are
more than the ego/mind that the "I" stands for when
*you say, "**I think** things will turn out okay". You are*
more than the emotions that the "I" stands for when
*you say, "**I feel** happy or sad today". And, likewise,*
you are more than the body that the "I" refers to when
*you say, "**I went** to town" or "**I stubbed** my toe."*
*The "I's" who **"think"**, and who **"feel"**, and who*
***"describe your physicality"** are vastly different*
from one another, and you need to learn to distinguish
between them.

Of course, in social situations or casual
conversation, you will still generally refer to the "I"
who relates to your body, your ego, or your feelings.
But within you, you serve yourselves well by knowing
that these "I's" do not represent the totality of who you
really are. They're the false "I's" that are temporary,

and that disappear when you leave this world. They're not eternal like the Spirit who lives on forever, the Spirit who you really are. Isn't it time you began to tell the truth about who you are, at least to yourself?

Lee Ching

How silly it was that you thought
you were something less than amazing,
that you were something less than immortal.
You've never been less than anything.

{Remember}
Oneness Is Our Next Step

I don't know about you, but when I'm brutally honest with myself, I have to recognize that life is very different than I thought it would be. When I was younger, I thought it was all about making a lot of money, or having the companionship of pretty women, or having a bunch of friends say, "Hey, you're really cool", etc. Of course, there's nothing wrong with these things, and, in fact, they can be great fun for a while, but that's not what life's all about. It's about knowing who I really am—and for that I have to learn *to hold my attention on my inner light for an extended period of time, long enough to rise up and out of the mainstream dream, and out of the illusion that I am my name, or that who I am has anything to do with where I grew up, or what I do for a living. In order to find out who I am at the center of my being, I have to let go of my entire story about myself; I have to let go of the assumption that I am separate from everyone and everything else in the world. I have to remember my connectedness, instead of my separateness...*

Noah Robinson

The underlying fabric of the world we live in is One. Some would say it's as if we're swimming through an unending sea of ever-changing life, like a fish swims through the ocean. Others liken it to a canvas upon which a beautiful work of art is painted. Still others would call it an all-pervading substance, a substance we don't see with our 3-D physical eyes, but a substance that exists behind the veil of our daily perceptions, nonetheless.

This fabric is made aware to us only when we let go of our tendency to see things separately from one another. Indeed, separation is the name of the game in 3-D, and in order to transcend it, and become aware of the One substance or underlying fabric, we'll need to look closer at the ways we separate the objects of this world from one another.

Look around you. If you're in a room, you see the objects within your sphere of vision: the tables and chairs, the walls, the floors, the ceiling, the toys and tools scattered about, the decorations here and there. These all appear to be separate and distinct from one another, but that is only how our five senses perceive them. Could there be another way to look at them?

Now let's look inside. In our ego/mind, we make all sorts of distinctions. We separate man from woman, one person from another, one group or party from another, one team from another, and so forth. Then, we take it a step further and place judgments on what we perceive, thinking things are good and bad, right and wrong, light and dark, hot and cold, you and me. Yes, we even make a separation between ourself and our fellow travelers, and we proceed to look for every little difference in our appearances, our behaviors, our preferences and tastes. These mental habits keep us separated all the more from one another.

Your ego is temporary, while your Spirit Essence is permanent. Your ego judges, holds grudges, harbors grievances, discriminates, hates, and separates—while your Spirit loves, honors, cares, serves, uplifts, forgives, and unifies. Your ego tethers you to the Earth time and time again, while your Spirit calls out through your soul for freedom. Your ego identifies with the body, while your Spirit identifies with All That Is, with Oneness, with God.

I go to a special place to get my drinking water from a nearby river. Most times when I'm there I run into a small, white haired man with a distinct twinkle in his eyes. I call him the mystery man and do not even know his real name (he tells me that the masters change their names all the time in order for us to be more comfortable with them so that they can get their messages across to us easier.) The names, he tells me, don't matter so much; what matters is the Spirit inside, and us coming into direct relationship with it.

I was filling my water jugs recently when he walked up and we began chatting, as usual. Typically, to get the conversation going, he finds a topic like gardening or what I've been doing lately, but on this day he skipped all the mundane topics and said something that's stuck with me ever since.

"You know, Tony, there's only one of us here." *he stated matter-of-factly. "I know that it looks like there's a whole lot of us traipsing around this world, but that's not really the case. It's much simpler than that. Everyone you see is you; you're always meeting yourself, no matter where you go or who you come in contact with. There's only one of us here, and the sooner you experience that for yourself, the happier you'll be."*

So, how do we dig our way out of all the layers of separation in order to get a glimpse of the Oneness that underlies it all? To be sure, there are many methods, and it takes a measure of practice. Some are solitary exercises, like meditation and prayer. However, one of the more popular methods in our western culture says, *"Anywhere two or more are gathered in My Name, there I shall be also."* This passage has been interpreted in many ways, referring to our becoming One with God. Said another way, when we experience the state of Oneness, we're experiencing God. These are the same experiences only with different names, and when this wondrous experience occurs, all separation between you and me melts away, all differences disappear entirely, all judgments subside, and what is left is a feeling inside us, a feeling like no other. It is this feeling that transcends all thinking. It is this feeling that reveals the underlying fabric of the One all-encompassing substance to us. It is this feeling that connects us to our Creator.

There isn't much about my days in the army that I remember, but one thing has stuck in my mind all these years—counting cadence. When we'd march together, we'd sing verses that kept us in step with one another, verses that typically ended with the words, "Sound Off - 1,2; Sound Off - 3,4; Sound Off 1,2,3,4,1,2 - 3,4!" These rhythmic verses have stuck with me throughout my life because that's when we were creating Oneness. You see, anytime you get a gathering of people together doing the same thing at the same time (like counting cadence), it creates Oneness. It doesn't matter whether it's in the military, at a sporting event, at a concert in the park, or in a church.

Oneness comes when people do things together.

— — —

*At the end of our Intenders circles, we always have a Oneness exercise. In other words, we set the stage for Oneness to occur. Over the years, we've found that Oneness is **the** spiritual experience, and we can't understand why most other spiritual and religious gatherings we've attended do not take a few minutes to do this when they come together. It's a simple matter to create an environment for everyone in the gathering to feel the Oneness, and it's a shame that this uplifting experience has been lost to so many.*

Here's how we do it: when all our intention and gratitude sharing is over, we all stand in a circle, hold hands, and tone ("Ahhhhh") or sing together. We do our best to be doing the same thing at the same time. Like a harmonic choir, we blend our voices, so that no one person is louder or more off-key than anyone else. Sometimes it takes a few moments for us to achieve this blending, but, when it happens, we can all feel it. That's when all our thoughts go away, typically our eyes close, and "a coming together" occurs ("anywhere two or more are gathered...").

**Whenever you tone together,
you're joined by the angels.**

In our circles, we tone long enough for this feeling to gel. Usually it happens within a couple of minutes, but sometimes—especially in groups who regularly practice this exercise—it happens right away. Then, after we stop our toning, we stand there, holding hands, and holding the silence for the same length of time that we toned. We do this because it's in this sweet silence that the feeling of Oneness is gelled even more. In fact, it feels so good that most of us don't want to move or leave the circle. Indeed, why would we?

You will be walking in the footsteps of angels, for you will be making them yourself.

You have sought long and hard to reach this place of Oneness with all things, and now a light shines in the distance and calls you to the pinnacle where your vistas expand and your true destiny awaits. You are no longer a child of the Earth; now you are a child of the Universe, spreading your newfound wings and ready to fly. And fly you shall. Indeed, you will soar beyond the mountains and valleys of this world, beyond the moon and stars, beyond this dimension and others to follow. Your Spirit is unlimited and all the Universe is open for your exploration. Adventures beyond your *wildest imaginings await now that you've left your old world behind. Now you're excited and expanded in all directions. Now you are free.*

Lee Ching

{Remember}
The Highest Good Will Set Us Free

Have the pure intention of everyone
awakening to the Highest Good.
That should be the intention
that is in the minds of everyone,
in the words of everyone,
and in the hearts of everyone, everywhere.

What if everyone in this world wanted only for the highest and best outcomes from all their endeavors? What if the Highest Good was taken into consideration in everything we do, in every intention we state, in every choice we make, with every person we meet? Let's envision it together, you and I, for just a moment.

In an environment where the Highest Good for one and all is honored, all life flourishes again, allowing men and women everywhere to pursue their life's purpose without intrusion. All guilt, all fear, all judgment, and all thoughts of wrongdoing have been replaced by our readiness to love and forgive our fellow travelers. Following this, the bell of our newfound freedom rings loud within us as our consciences awaken, our compassion blossoms, and our communication with one another becomes clear and true.

With the Highest Good in place, there's no hunger, no disease, no scarcity or shortage of any kind because we're all sharing whatever we have with our friends and neighbors, knowing that whatever we share comes back to us tenfold. Fear in all its ugly disguises is a thing of the past since all living souls have access to everything they need to enjoy happy, fulfilled lives. Our Mother Earth shines again now that human selfishness has vanished in the wake of the Highest Good. Wars have ended, poverty is gone, all debts are forgiven. Zero point energy to power our homes, our workplaces, and our transportation is free for all. No more do we spoil our air, our soil, our waters; no more do we waste our precious resources; no more do our beautiful animals have to hide now that we have stopped harming them.

For so long we'd been kept quarantined from the rest of the cosmos because of our violent nature. However, the minute we agreed to honor the Highest Good, the path to the stars opened wide before us. Now our ancient ancestors from across the Universe call us back into the fold to share their wisdom, their stories, their technologies, their love.

And now, as that love is freely shared, our quarantine is lifted, our hearts open wide, and we step forth into our highest calling, our greatest destiny—a destiny that promises all the wonders and joys of new life, new expansion, and new opportunities in worlds once forgotten and now revealed. We are welcomed with open arms by our ancient family who have long awaited our return, who have long intended for us, one and all, to realign with the Highest Good.

If we really want it, we have to live it now.

Review

One afternoon as I was intending for a thread to bring the ideas in this book together, I suddenly had the phrases in *The Highest Good Guides poster* come into my mind. They were so positive that I kept saying them over and over, and, in the days that followed, I realized that they had an order to them, starting with the more physically-oriented ideas and ending with the more spiritual perspectives. As I continued to connect these positive phrases to the Highest Good, I also inserted favorites from my collection of inspiring Intenders stories to bring more fun and greater clarity to the book. In the process, several common themes began to stand out in the writing, creating the thread I was intending for all along. In fact, let's go over these recurring themes as a review, so you can come back and refer to them anytime you like.

1.) We have a calling, a purpose for being here. When we find out what our calling is, everything falls into place for us because we're doing what we came here to do. By the same token, when we stray from our calling, we step out of the flow of life, and challenges are more apt to present themselves.

2.) It's all an inside job. In order to fix the world, we first have to fix ourselves. Our challenges are all in our mind, and that's the place where the work starts. Within.

3.) The best tools for lining up with the Highest Good are love and forgiveness—but not the old way of forgiveness. Instead, we utilize *the new forgiveness,* which sees only innocence and compassion. No wrongdoing, judging, or blaming are involved.

4.) *The new forgiveness,* in the wise words of Jesus in A Course in Miracles, *"is still, and quietly does nothing ... It merely looks, and waits, and judges not." (ACIM)* He says we can simply *"overlook"* all thoughts of guilt and wrongness, and remain calm and still whenever they arise.

5.) In the face of aggressive people, all parties

involved are best served when we restrain our tendency to fight back; when we forgive others, and offer them *"lilies instead of thorns."* For it's when we offer blessings and beneficence to others and see them in their Highest Light that we set the wheels in motion for them to reconsider and change their violent ways. We remember that all other approaches for bringing peace into our personal lives and into our world have not worked, and will never work. We must love others if we want love returned.

6.) *Love* is what lies beyond *Life, Liberty, and the Pursuit of Happiness*. It's the one item the Founding Fathers left out, and it is time, now, for us to include *Love* as we seek to embody the Highest Good.

7.) Four Universal Laws: *Attraction, Agreement, Cause and Effect,* and *Diminishing Returns* have been brought up many times throughout this book because of their vital importance to our well-being. The *Law of Attraction* says that our physical world is first created in our thoughts, in our mind. It's the foundation upon which we build our future experiences. It reminds us to pay closer attention to what we're thinking and saying, lest we attract *miscreations* into our lives. The *Law of Agreement* protects us from unwanted experiences and from others who would have us do their bidding. It asks us to discern and withhold our agreement from any issues we don't want to be reinforcing or manifesting. The *Law of Cause and Effect* tells us that whatever we sow, so shall we reap. It cautions us to be more aware of what we're thinking and creating, and to consider whether we would want to "live out" the effects of the creations we're causing. The *Law of Diminishing Returns* acts to keep our health and relationships in balance by reminding us to *consciously* take regular breaks from our habits and routines.

8.) In applying these laws in your own life, you are reminded to ask yourself if what you're thinking about, what you're talking about, or what you're listening to others talk about will serve you and your fellow travelers. Will it give you the outcomes and results you're intending for? To be in complete alignment with the Highest Good, you will need to be asking yourself these important questions moment to moment throughout the day. *The answers you receive will determine whether you're creating or miscreating.*

9.) The fine points of making and manifesting your intentions are included herein to help you get where you want to go in life. Learning to both envision and feel your intentions having already manifested will accelerate your inner work, so you'll be better able to do your work out in the world when the time comes. Getting proficient with these tools will increase your ability to experience all the joy and fulfillment this life has to offer.

10.) Trust replaces worry. It's the little things that we intend for and manifest in the course of our daily lives that build our level of trust. Every time we consciously bring our everyday wants and needs into manifestation, our trust in the intention-making process grows. But, as we're learning, we have to remember to state our intentions in the first place.

11.) The road to our personal and collective

happiness lies not in separation or opposition, but in coming together in Oneness. No matter where we are, we can set the stage for Oneness to occur; we can learn to cultivate the feeling of Oneness with others, with our world, and with our Creator.

12.) Finally, you can take the information in this book that's applicable to you and use it for yourself. It will help you understand your life better. In time, your life will change into the vision offered in these pages. As Lee Ching told us long ago, *"The Highest Good is your saving grace..."* But you must use it. You must apply it everyday. It doesn't serve you to put it off for another time. You must live it now, and it will bring you all the *Love, Life, Liberty, and Happiness* you could ever intend for.

Be the ideal.
Be all the Love that's within you.
Be the Highest Good.

213

A Fun Final Exam

T F 1. Your experiences are directly related to your thoughts.

T F 2. Your desires are in you to be fulfilled.

T F 3. Some people are more deserving of abundance than others.

T F 4. What you're looking for is what you are looking with.

T F 5. Living your calling lines you up with the Highest Good.

T F 6. You live only once.

T F 7. The doctor is always right.

T F 8. You can't have any effect on the world around you.

T F 9. The last step in intending is letting go.

T F 10. You've been innocent since the day you were born.

T F 11. For every point of view, its opposite is equally valid.

T F 12. What you say is what you get.

13. The best way to deal with an enemy or adversary is:
A: offer them "lilies instead of thorns."
B: see them in their Highest Light
C: forgive them
D: All of the above

14. Your thoughts can make you:
A: Happy
B: Sick
C: Abundant
D: All of the above

15. Happiness is to be found in:
A: Opposition
B: Separation
C: Coming together
D: Being aloof

16. We're aligned with the Highest Good when we:
A: stand for *win-win*
B: care for others
C: love every living creature
D: All of the above

17. Immoderation affects our:

A: Health

B: Relationships

C: Work environment

D: All of the above

18. The best place to resolve our problems is:

A: At the bank

B: In our mind

C: At home

D: In a hot tub

19. The Highest Good is best served by:

A: Blaming others

B: Judging others

C: Forgiving others

D: Assigning guilt

20. To fix the world, we must:

A: Become an activist

B: First make a lot of money

C: First fix ourself

D: Get a college degree

21. The Highest Good:
A: Always sends us in the right direction
B: Is our saving grace
C: Can cause temporary discomfort
D. All of the above

22. We transmute unwanted experiences by:
A: Nipping our negative thoughts in the bud
B: Envisioning only positive outcomes
C: Staying in the here and now
D: All of the above

23. A miscreation:
A: Brings undesired outcomes
B: Is born out of love
C: Serves everyone concerned
D. Always provides great results

24. Our ego/mind:
A: is judgmental
B: holds grudges
C: seeks revenge
D: All of the above

25. We're forgiving when we:
A: Are quiet and still
B: No longer judging
C: Witnessing impartially
D: All of the above

Do you stand for the Highest Good?

The Intenders are honored to award our **Certificate of Alignment with The Highest Good** to those who correctly answer at least 22 of the questions above. If you stand for the Highest Good and you passed our Fun Final Exam, it entitles you to become an official Intenders *Ambassador for the Highest Good* and to act on behalf of the Highest Good in everything you do, in every intention you state, in every choice you make, with every person you meet.

You can receive your free Award Certificate at: *http://www.highestlighthouse.com/award.html*

Answers: 1T 2T 3F 4T 5T 6F 7F 8F 9T 10T 11T 12T 13D 14D 15C 16D 17D 18B 19C 20C 21D 22D 23A 24D 25D

Certificate of Alignment
with the

HIGHEST GOOD

This is to certify that

TERRIE HALEY

has fulfilled all requirements and is now recognised as being in total alignment with the Highest Good. Let it be known to all concerned parties that the recipient of this award carries the pure intention of all people everywhere awakening and aligning with the Highest Good.

All award recipients are entitled to become official Ambassadors for the Highest Good and are intending to act on behalf of the Highest Good in everything they do, in every choice they make, with every person they meet.

So be it and so it is!

signature

The Inventor of the Highest Good

Date: 4/26/18

Gratitude

This book has been a life-long process in coming, a labor of love every step of the way. I'm honored to have been a part of it, and I would like to thank the people who have helped bring it into manifestation. First, my neverending gratitude goes out to Tina Stober, Lee Ching, and BJ. You have changed my life in too many ways to mention here. I love you and thank you for showing me what caring is all about.

I would also like to thank my Houston brother, Dan Hunter, who happened along at just the right time (when I was intending for direction) to bring the ideas herein into focus. Likewise, I am extremely grateful to Thomas and Merel Marschall, Gary Frierdich, and everyone in my Pagosa family for their friendship and loving support. Without Dan, Tom, Merel and Gary, this book would not be what it is today, nor would I.

There are many Intenderpreneurs who contributed in different ways to this work, although five of them stand out: Leigh Morano in Des Moines, IA, Anne Whigham in Spokane, WA, Gayle Abrams in Palatka, FL, Pam Baugh in Redding, CA, and Hazel Martin in

Edinburgh, Scotland. Each of you has inspired me more than you'll ever know. Blessed be you.

I also express my gratitude to Terrie Haley, Akron, OH Intenderpreneur who is responsible for creating the beautiful graphics on the uplifting *"Highest Good Guides"* Poster and the *Award Certificate* that accompany this book. Thank you, Terrie.

To Intenders everywhere who have stood steadfast for the Highest Good all these years: You are my inspiration and I intend that all the intentions you have made on behalf of the Highest Good come to you tenfold and more.

And last but not least, to you, friendly reader —may you take what you have learned from this work and, starting within, manifest a life and a world for yourself that is so unimaginably grand and glorious that you barely recognize it in comparison to where you stand today.

Tony Burroughs

May all your intentions be for the Highest Good and may all your dreams come true.
So be it and so it is.
It is done!

About the Intenders

Over the last twenty-five years, the Intenders of the Highest Good have helped people all over the world integrate the Intention Process into their daily lives, both individually and in community. Embodied in the Intenders information is a call to take our next step in life, and it provides us with the free tools to do it. *The Code, The Bridge, The Intenders Circle, The Law of Agreement, The Vision Alignment Project, The Intention Process* and *The Ascension Process* are all models for uplifting the individual and the group—and, at the same time, lining everyone up with the Highest Good.

For more information about the Intenders,
you can go to:

www.intenders.com,
www.highestlighthouse.com,
www.intenders.org,
www.visionalignmentproject.com
and www.tonyburroughs.net
Intenders Book Orders: Call 858-200-5200.

About the Author

Tony Burroughs is one of the more prolific visionaries of our time. He is an inspired storyteller, the author of 12 self-empowerment books, and is the cofounder of the Intenders of the Highest Good, a grassroots community movement with Intenders Circles in countries all over the world. His widely acclaimed *Vision Alignment Project* recently surpassed 2.5 million alignments. He has produced 3 full-length videos, over 130 YouTubes for the Intenders Channel, and has appeared on numerous TV and radio shows, including Coast to Coast AM. His last book, *The Ascenders Handbook; Two Roads Home*, is the long awaited sequel to his bestseller, *The Intenders Handbook,* while this book, *The Highest Good Handbook: Love, Life, Liberty and the Pursuit of Happiness* is filled with powerful stories that influenced Tony and other Intenders along the way. When he's not traveling to Intenders Circles around the country, Tony lives in Pagosa Springs, Colorado.

Intenders Books, Ebooks, CDs, and DVDs
by Tony Burroughs

The Highest Good Handbook:
Love, Life, Liberty and the Pursuit of Happiness
What You Need To Know Now: Lee Ching Messages
Get What You Want:
The Art of Making and Manifesting Your Intentions
The Intenders Handbook: A Guide to the Intention
Process and the Conscious Community
The Highest Light Teachings
The Ascenders Handbook: Two Roads Home
The Law of Agreement
The Code: 10 Intentions for a Better World
I See A World: Best of the Vision Alignment Project
WINS: Manifestation Stories from the Intenders
The Code 2: The Reunion: A Parable for Peace
The Intenders of the Highest Good: A Novel

—

The Intention Process DVD:
How to Start Your Own Intention Circle
A Guide for Conscious Manifestation
and Community Making
On the Road with the Code (2-DVD or 3-CD Set)
Living by Manifesting (3-DVD or 3-CD Set)